JERUSALEM'S GLORY

First published, London, 1661.

By Thomas Watson, a lover of peace.

"(For not the hearers of the law *are* just before God, but the doers of the law shall be justified. For when the Gentiles, which have not the law, do by nature the things contained in the law, these, having not the law, are a law unto themselves: Which shew the work of the law written in their hearts, their conscience also bearing witness, and *their* thoughts the mean while accusing or else excusing one another;)" (Romans 2:13-15).

JERUSALEM'S GLORY

Thomas Watson

*A Puritan's view of
what the church should be*

Edited by
Roger N McDermott M.A. (Oxon)

Christian Heritage

Roger N McDermott is a graduate of the University of Oxford and an historian. He has written for the New Dictionary of National Biography, as well as contributing historical articles to The Banner of Truth Magazine and Evangelical Times. He is also the editor of a range of puritan titles for Christian Focus Publications. He lives in Kent with his wife Melanie.

Introduction © Roger McDermott

ISBN 1 85792 569 6

Published in 2002 by
Christian Focus Publications
Geanies House, Fearn, Ross-shire
Great Britain IV20 1TW

www.christianfocus.com

Cover design by Alister MacInnes.

Printed and Bound by
MFP Design & Print, Manchester

Contents

Editor's Dedication

———————

For My Wife Melanie

INTRODUCTION

The puritans have a deserved place of honour in the history of the Christian Church as a godly and self-effacing people. Their work and writings come to the modern reader as a refreshing dose of spiritual honesty in a world so beset by spiritual darkness and deceit. In fact they provide wholesome food for the soul of the hungry Christian. The Israelites in the days of Moses were provided with Manna to eat, and they called it 'Manna' since they 'wist not what it *was*' (Exodus 16:15). But Christ declared himself in the fullness of time to be 'the bread of life' who offers real nourishment to the souls of those who feed on him, by faith (John 6:35).

The success of the puritans lay in their recognition of Jesus Christ as the only appointed mediator of the New Covenant, and as Head, King, Saviour and Lord of his own Church. They placed Him who is 'a chief cornerstone' (I Peter 2:6) at the very centre of their worship, doctrine, preaching and way of life. To a fallen and sin-sick world they unashamedly proclaimed 'Christ-crucified' as the only God given way of salvation.

It can only be a false religion that does not confront the problem of man's sin and rebellion with the impending Judgement of the Holy and Living God and the way of salvation through the atonement of the Eternal and only-begotten Son of God, Jesus Christ. The religion of the puritans was true religion. It was Reformed and stood on the sure and certain ground of the word of God; it was also a heart felt religion that aimed at the glory of God. To achieve this meant avoiding lightness and trivia in the worship of God and cultivating holiness in the daily life of every Christian. In other words, puritan belief was implemented in practice.

The following book, *Jerusalem's Glory,* written in 1661 by Thomas Watson, contains all the hallmarks of what made the puritans great. It represents a clarion call to the Church to recognize her waywardness and repent, turning to the Almighty God and casting herself on His mercy. Its author did not employ 'enticing words of man's wisdom,' (I Corinthians 2:4) but sought to apply biblical truth and sound doctrine as a means to achieving the stated aim. Here we gain some insight into the virtue of a puritan preacher of the gospel, speaking plainly to the ills of society, and in particular to the Church, that according to the Scriptures is 'a city that is set on an hill' (Matthew 5:14).

But what was so wrong with society that it required such sharp rebuke? And in what way had the Church gone astray in 17th century England? Against the background of so much godly preaching in puritan England, did not the Church show signs of progress and even of greater unity? In order to answer these questions it is worthwhile remembering the condition of society and the Church at the time, and in particular the context in which the work was first published. It is also important to establish the credentials of Watson as the author of the text, in offering his critique of the spiritual malaise that was spreading far and wide, almost crippling the health and witness of the Church. Finally, it must be shown what bearing the author's work continues to have in our day.

England witnessed great changes and enormous conflict during the 17th century. Politically conflict and war marred it; disputes were increasingly contributing to an atmosphere of hostility and hatred. But important issues were at stake as the conflict between crown and parliament was played out. The issue of liberty featured prominently, ever since the fragile Tudor balance in Church and State was destabilized by the ascendance to the throne of James I in 1603. His brand of kingship and distaste for parliament seemed to pose an open threat to the liberty of the subject. Charles I carried this to an extreme, as the issue of 'crown rights,' came to dominate the minds of men.

No one seriously doubted that kings ruled by the authority of God, however the practical application of that was a matter of sharp division. The constitutional unity of the nation was fractured for a time as men divided into 'Royalists' and 'Parliamentarians.' The bloody and cruel civil wars that ensued in England affected the whole of the British Isles. Wars are never regarded as a desirable way of settling disputes, even less so in the case of a civil war.

Charles I had not desired war, what the Stuart ruler struggled so desperately to achieve was a uniformity of the multiple kingdoms which he ruled over. The great liberty that the British people knew in the period, was their historical deliverance from the tyranny of Rome. The Reformation of the Church was the singularly most important blessing enjoyed among the people; the gospel of Jesus Christ was giving true liberty to souls. The Stuart monarchs endeavoured in the pursuit of their own power to undermine this liberty; the drift back toward Rome was both slow and insidious.

To achieve uniformity within the Church, in 1637 Charles I imposed a Prayer Book on the English model on the Scots. This was far removed from Knox's *Book of Common Order*. The rejection of it the following year signalled the signing of the National Covenant. Shortly after the Bishops Wars confirmed the failure of royal policy, with the Scots calling for the abolition of Episcopacy in Scotland. Before too long, the same demand was made within the English Parliament.

The times called loudly for resolute men, strong in the faith and relying solely upon the Living God, to contend for the faith. That was certainly visible in the gathering of the puritan divines at the Westminster Assembly between 1643-6. Of those, Baxter contended that the world had not known such a gathering of eminent godly men, since the Council of Jerusalem in the first century.

Thomas Watson did not seem a particularly brilliant man to his contemporaries. Yet he earned their respect as a godly preacher of the gospel. A serious and diligent man, he emerged from relative obscurity to a certain prominence within the Church that brought him into conflict with the enemies of the gospel. Perhaps as the Scriptures record of David, the greatest accolade that Watson may be given is to say that 'he had served his own generation by the will of God' (Acts 13:36).

Born in Yorkshire between 1617-19, information on the early life of Watson is markedly scarce. When he was of age, he went to Emmanuel College, Cambridge, in 1635. There he gained a reputation as a very industrious student, achieving his B.A. in 1638-9 and proceeding to M.A. in 1642. The timing of Watson's conversion is not known, but on his arrival at Emmanuel College he would have had in theory an express interest in the ministry of the gospel. For it will be remembered that Emmanuel was set up in the 16th century to provide the Church with educated and godly ministers. By 1635, the college was flourishing as a centre of godly learning, and a 'hotbed' of puritan activity. Many of the great puritans were educated at the University of Cambridge, such as, Cartwright, Perkins, Sibbes, and Charnock, to name but a few. In particular, at Emmanuel, eminent divines were raised up by God to further the cause of Christ in the nation. Not least of these was John Preston, appointed as Master of Emmanuel in 1622. The value of his written work was highly regarded by many fellow puritan ministers, among whom Richard Sibbes and John Davenport tirelessly edited the works of Preston after the death of the latter in 1628. These works included, *The New Covenant, The Golden Sceptre*, and perhaps more widely known, *The Breastplate of Faith and Love*.

The influence of Preston at Emmanuel cannot be overstated. His stance as both a puritan and presbyterian did much to lay the groundwork for the growth of presbyterianism within the Church of England and beyond. It was in that godly environment that Thomas Watson was educated, and it is of little surprise to find him later fully committed to the presbyterian model of Church government.

The year of Watson's entry to Cambridge did not seem unusually significant. It saw the development of a postal service in England. It also saw increasing conflict in both Church and state, through the activity of William Laud and Charles I. Parliament had not met in England since the king had prorogued it in 1628. All of the dissension spreading throughout the country revolved around a struggle for the preservation of liberty and justice. Not least did this express itself in the Church, which seemed to many to be in danger of drifting back toward Romanism, and declining from the standards of the 16th century Reformation.

As the years of study passed for Watson at Cambridge these problems on the wider front were reaching a critical stage. Archbishop Laud had destabilized the fragile political balance throughout the British Isles by his innovative ecclesiastical practices and his espousal of Arminian heresy. Charles I seemed to share his Archbishop's enthusiasm for Arminianism, but rapidly sought to distance himself from this position after the downfall of the former. Parliament was forced to oppose the errant and inflexible monarch, and in 1642, the first civil war erupted in England.

At precisely this time Watson emerged from his studies, proceeding to his M.A. in 1642. By that time he was no doubt eager to begin his pastoral ministry, but God had other plans for him. God used the interest in personal correspondence generated by the development of the postal service in 1635, as a means to guiding his servant. In another part of the country, in Castle Hedingham, Essex, the godly Mary Tracey, Lady Vere, wife of Horatio Vere, was busy forming links with puritan ministers. Indeed the historical record bears witness of her friendships with many eminent divines, corresponding with William Ames, John Dod, Obadiah Sedgewick,

Richard Sibbes and Thomas Watson. Lady Vere did much to help godly ministers, especially in times of distress and persecution, she also promoted the advancement of godly men into vacant churches.

Between 1642-46 Watson resided in the household of Lady Vere, and patiently waited on God's timing of his entry to the ministry. One other woman that he had to meet before taking up his first church, was a woman of whom less is known, but who undoubtedly also influenced him for good; her name was Abigail Beadle, the daughter of another puritan, John Beadle, minister in Barnston, Essex. In 1646, Watson married Abigail in Barnston, and shortly afterward he entered the ministry. Ordained as a clerk at St. Stephen's, Walbrook in London in 1646, he continued preaching there until his ejection from the Church of England as a consequence of the Act of Uniformity in 1662, which witnessed the Great Ejection of around 2,000 puritan ministers of the gospel.

Amidst the grand surroundings of the ornate interior of St Stephen's, later re-designed by Sir Christopher Wren, Watson proclaimed the whole counsel of God, preaching simply and to the hearts of his hearers. In those years his written ministry also flourished. These included *The Art of Divine Contentment, The Christians Charter, The Beatitudes,* and *Jerusalem's Glory.*

In the Providence of God, Watson was brought into severe testing of his convictions during the early part of his ministry. He was among a group of Presbyterian ministers who presented a remonstrance to Oliver Cromwell and the Council of War, protesting against the execution of the king in 1649. Later in 1651 he was involved with a number of other men in the 'Love plot' to bring Charles II to England and restore the monarchy. For his pains he spent four months in the Tower of London, released after petitioning for mercy. But he was later tested in a much more personal way when called on to decide on the impending Act of Uniformity.

Shortly after the Restoration of Charles II in 1660, the initial euphoria and the high hopes of many puritans for a settlement of the divisions of the Church gave way to more sober views. The government was moving swiftly toward enacting intolerant legislation that would apparently resolve the disunity of the Church. The puritans were regarding the situation with increasing concern. All the signs of growing intolerance toward sound doctrine and true religion were noted with alarm among the godly. The Church having swung one way, then another, being dogged by Arminianism under the misguided leadership of Archbishop Laud, and afterward taking steps towards compelling the uniform observance of the Book of Common Prayer in the Church of England, seemed in the grip of another departure from the truth of the gospel. This was all in the name of unity, or rather uniformity, as monarchy and ecclesiastical leaders cooperated in achieving a forced 'peace' within the Church.

In April 1661, the second Savoy Conference was called, in an effort to find such a peace for the divided Church. Many were skeptical, and were soon proven correct in their assessment of the intentions of those pursuing the policies of the Restoration Church. The Savoy Conference considered the objections of the puritans to the Prayer Book. It consisted of 12 representatives on either side, each with a number of assistants. Among the Episcopal delegates, were Frewin, Archbishop of York, Sheldon, Bishop of London, and Cosin, Bishop of Durham. The puritan delegation included Manton, Reynolds, and Baxter. Despite the efforts of the puritans, the conference did little to heal the divisions opening up within the Church; in fact the Bishops had fixed the outcome against their opponents. As Bayne later reflected on the outcome of the conference, saying, 'the yoke of the ceremonies is not relaxed by a jot or a tittle.'

The undoubted aim of the puritans at the Savoy Conference was to promote true unity among all Protestants. They drew up a list of objections to the Book of Common Prayer. They asked that the gift of prayer be permitted to continue without hindrance; called for the abolition of readings from the Apocrypha; the Authorized Version of the Bible, 1611, should be used exclusively; the term, 'minister' should replace 'priest;' the power to exclude Christians from the sacrament of the Lord's Supper when under the discipline of the Church, should lie with the minister; and greater explanation of the doctrines of the Reformed Faith included in the Catechism. The Episcopal authorities duly declined these.

The godly had faithfully discharged their duties under God, the truth of which was attested to by Baxter in his autobiography, 'England had been like in a quarter of an age to have become a land of saints and a pattern of holiness to the world, and the unmatchable paradise of the earth. Never were such fair opportunities to sanctify a nation lost and trodden underfoot as have been in this land of late. Woe be to them that are the causes of it.'

As the Savoy Conference was still in session, the 'Cavalier' Parliament was called in May 1661. Here Clarendon began the process leading to the passing of the Act of Uniformity the following year. At the opening of that Parliament, the Lord Chancellor referred to the puritans as 'seditious preachers.' The hatred toward the godly was much in evidence, but perhaps of greater concern was the act of publicly burning the Solemn League and Covenant, which the King had taken on oath several times. The promises of the King lay in tatters; his word to God and his subjects were openly flouted.

At precisely this time Thomas Watson, in the spring of 1661, published the following work. Shortly afterwards he and many other puritans, were called upon to publicly react to the passing of the Act of Uniformity, in 1662. They chose to obey God rather than men, and the Great Ejection that ensued is adequate testimony of their convictions and their love of the truth.

Recognizing the spiritual ailments of his day, as well as the possibility of separation that lay ahead, Watson was principally concerned for the spiritual welfare of Christians, and in particular his own congregation. He loved those people, faithfully ministering to their needs for many years; above all they required leadership and direction at a time of general confusion. In *Jerusalem's Glory* these are the pre-eminent features: a pastor's care for his own flock, and indeed for the wider Church.

The original subtitle to the book provides further evidence as to the author's motives in writing the work, *The Saints' safety in Eyeing the Church's Security.* The chief concern of the author was that of the safety of the saints; he is concerned with the wellbeing of true Christians. But safety in what? In 'eyeing,' or considering the security of the Church, for that security is promised to her by the Living and true God. This message of comfort was especially required during the affliction that the Church was under at the time. To offer any durable comfort the message itself had to address difficult and serious issues, it also had to remind the people of God of His dealings with his people in former times. It is clear from the text that Watson believed certain things that were wrong in the Church had to be put right, in order that God would bless His Church. But what was so terribly wrong in the Church?

1. *Disunity* within the Church was sadly on the increase. Disunity in the Church is always a

product of *error*. The denominations of the Reformed churches were often unable to display genuine Christian unity among them. Independents disagreed with Presbyterians and Episcopalians were divided against each other as well as other denominations. Watson could recollect the unseemly spectacle of the godly in Scotland and England taking up arms against one another during the civil war. The various conferences such as the Hampton Court Conference of 1604 or the Savoy Conferences later in the century brought no resolution to the existing ecclesiastical division. A marked level of disunity continued even after the meeting of the Divines at the Westminster Assembly between 1643-46, which certainly arrived at a basis for Church unity, however much ignored.

2. *Declension* from the truth of the gospel was a common feature of life in the Church in the author's experience. As suggested above this was the twin sister of disunity. It reared its ugly head by means of churchmen holding erroneous views concerning the validity of tradition as well as the Scriptures as the basis of authority in the Church. The reformers and puritans held that the Scriptures alone constituted the court of final appeal in all matters of controversy in religion: once this was

subverted the floodgates were opened for declension in the purity of the doctrine, worship and discipline of the Church.

3. Innovation in the worship of God went hand in hand with the declension from sound doctrinal truth. The Laudian party devoted their energy to the beautification of the Church, for whom the externals of worship such as surplices or altarpieces were very important. The puritan party of course, saw these externals as the mere vestiges of Romanism, with all its appeal to the senses and the natural man. In fact their continued presence within the Church of England provided the main grounds of the puritan call for the further reformation of the Church. The Church was in danger of losing her way, drifting away from the standards of the Reformation; consequently almost any novel idea from leading churchmen gained acceptance in the worship of God. Against this innovative spirit the puritans stood together on the principle that God alone has commanded in His own word how He will be worshipped: all else stems from the corruption of our nature and equates with idolatry, which is forbidden by God.

4. Man-centred and outward religion became popular once again, despite the blessing of the 16th century Reformation. Monarchy and prelates cooperated in the promulgation of unbiblical practices in the Church that placed its emphasis on the outward and visible. The wearing of the surplice was one of a host of examples. Heart religion was being rapidly shunned as an embarrassment and a needless thing. Arminianism required like Romanism, the giddy appeal to the senses of outward show and pomp. In the early 1660's the Laudian party were triumphing in the Church.

5. *Covenant Breaking,* was perhaps the most dramatic feature of what was wrong in the Church. In 1643 the 'Solemn League and Covenant,' was 'approved by the General Assembly of the Church of Scotland, and by both Houses of Parliament, and the Assembly of Divines in England.' The breach of this National Covenant was possibly the greatest act of treachery in the history of these Isles; its repudiation by Charles II in 1661 presaged the bitter persecution of the Covenanters in Scotland.

The answer to these ills in the Church presented by the author may be summarized as follows. Watson begins by briefly considering the condition of the people of God during the Babylonian captivity as expressed by the sacred writer in Psalm 137. Here God's people were found suffering under the affliction of the Babylonians, and in such a condition they could only cry out to

God for deliverance. It was a painful and bitter experience and is recorded in the Scriptures for the instruction of the Church in all ages.

The afflicting hand of God was upon the Church, and its cause lay in the sin of the people. God could not bless His Church until it had been dealt with; rooted out and repented of in the lives and practice of His own people. Of course this was not new in the history of the Israelites, for they could easily recall the occasion of the sin of Achan in the camp: equally in that instance God required the sin to be confronted and dealt with.

Watson deals at length with the issue of Christians being marked out as those whose promises are carried through in their daily lives. They ought to be covenant keepers rather than covenant breakers, note how far he carries this in chapter 8. The Church of his day had broken its loyalty toward the God of the Covenant in so many ways and had to be warned of the consequences of these actions. There could be no circumventing the serious problems of the Church, from her divisions to her declension from the truth. Christ would maintain His controversy with the Church and demand repentance. As another puritan, Richard Rogers, once confessed, 'I serve an exact God.'

There was no easy route to unity and spiritual

prosperity on offer from the preacher of St. Stephen's; no soothsaying nor false comfort for those 'that are at ease in Zion' (Amos 6:1). The route outlined in *Jerusalem's Glory* is an old, well-trodden path: well trodden that is by the saints of God. True unity lay in true religion exemplified by a life lived in vital union with Christ; it was a lesson learned historically time and again by the people of God.

In a time of national and ecclesiastical declension from God, the puritans were painfully aware that 'righteousness exalteth a nation, but sin is a reproach to any people' (Proverbs 14:34). That message was relentlessly proclaimed by the puritans, who reminded man of his duty before God, and the Christian duty of the obedience of faith.

It is a seminal lesson from the history of the Church that can only be ignored at incalculable cost to Christians. Our modern generation knows much of sin, but less of its awful consequences; far less still of righteousness. Worldliness and a sickening appetite for pleasure, self-seeking and innovation too infect the Church. The departure of national churches from the standards of the Bible and true religion is everywhere in evidence. This spiritual malaise, exacerbated by apathy, is invading many of the churches that lay claim to be Reformed. Men are filling our pulpits whose spinelessness prevents them from proclaiming the whole counsel of God. The Achan's of the modern Church have become innumerable.

But blessed is the God of our fathers, who will be praised from generation to generation, that He has raised up a standard against evil. A faithful few are still by the grace of God proclaiming the eternal truth of the gospel of Jesus Christ. Watson as already noted, 'served his own generation by the will of God,' he faithfully laboured for its spiritual and moral improvement through the gospel. Today his writings continue in the same vein, being an influence on their readers for good. In this spirit, this work of Thomas Watson, long out of print, is wholeheartedly commended to the reader. Look beyond its author and the historical context, to the Eternal and unchanging God; search the Scriptures, and establish for yourself whether these things are so. And if on reading the work you come to share the author's depth of conviction, then act upon this by living a godly life and by enjoying God now. Labour also, as Watson did, for the Reformation of the Church; putting right the things that are wrong and offensive to God. Do not content yourself with knowledge of the truth, and a mere outward show in religion, but close in with God in Christ and show your love for Him through obeying His commands.

Almost a century earlier, the Genevan reformer John Calvin commented on the love toward the Church that every believer ought to have: 'The Lord's people, while they mourn under personal trials, should be still more deeply affected by the public calamities which befall the Church, it being reasonable that the zeal of God's house should have the highest place in our hearts, and rise above all mere private considerations.' This expresses the sentiment of the inspired Psalmist and the people of God, during the Babylonian Captivity that forms the subject of Psalm 137. As the New Testament Church was foreshadowed in the Old Testament, there are clear lessons for the Christian Church that deserve close attention. Sin within the camp must be purged out. This is true of the Church, as well as the individual believer. To seek the blessing of God upon His Church, first entails our corporate and individual reformation; then God will return in His infinite mercy, to bless His Church.

The life and work of Watson after the first publication of this text in 1661 and his ejection from the National Church the following year, is a model of godliness and spirituality. He faithfully laboured in the ministry of an independent Presbyterian Chapel in Crosby Square, London, and was later joined there by Stephen Charnock as co-pastor between 1675-80. His written works that became so highly valued include *A Body of Divinity* (an exposition of the shorter catechism), *Heaven Taken by Storm* and *Religion Our True Interest.* But at the heart of Watson's religion was a personal and experiential knowledge of Jesus Christ, denoted by his individual holiness and love for the truth of the gospel. Two brief examples will sufficiently convey this.

Calamy recorded the instance of the author's meeting with Bishop Richardson prior to 1662, who was so impressed by the preaching and public prayer of Watson that he requested a copy of the prayer. Watson replied, 'Alas! That is what I cannot give, for I do not use to pen my prayers; it was no studied thing, but uttered *pro re natta,* as God enabled, from the abundance of my heart and affections.' Neither in preaching nor in praying did Watson rely on a dry outward form of words. Finally, Calamy also provides evidence of his closing in with God in prayer, noting the passing of the author at Barnston, Essex in 1686 whilst engaging in prayer: a fitting and noble testimony to his practical Christianity.

Let us then clearly follow the Scriptures in these things. The Church cries out in her affliction for the downfall of all false religion and the prosperity of true religion. The epitome of false religion is of course found in Rome, the great mystical Babylon; but the triumph of Christ and His Church is assured. The American Presbyterian, Plumer, writing in the early 19th century commented on this, 'How glorious will be the final triumph of the Church over her great adversary, the mystical Babylon, when the loud cry of the mighty angel shall be heard, "Babylon the great is fallen, is fallen!" (Rev. 18:2). But let every idol and the vestiges of false religion be first rooted out of our own hearts: for the praise and glory of Jesus Christ. To that aim and the furtherance of true Church unity, may the words of Thomas Watson be a source of encouragement.

Roger McDermott

JERUSALEM'S
GLORY

PREFACE

I offer the following observations to you, seeking your most serious consideration on what I have written; if it is nothing more to you than was previously known, do not reject it, nor despise the day of small things. But rather rejoice to see the same light shine in me, as you prize in yourself; and know that he that goes up to Heaven by Jacob's ladder, must not treat the first step with contempt.

Suppose this small book should not meet with acceptance among your collection, but it may seem entirely opposed to your more usual reading. Yet seeing I have revealed my mind to you so freely, hoping to involve you in the circumference of my love, than to render you the object of my envy. Let it suffice, to pass by those things that may seem opposed to your understanding, and rashly conclude, that all things which are difficult, must assuredly be false. Or imagining a wrong interpretation, or even ignorance in my writing; many things may seem fashionable to you, in your current preoccupations, which if they were brought to the touch-stone of Christ and His apostles, would prove no better than an opinion held by custom or tradition, rather than from the real grounds of Scripture.

Even so, it is very probable, that several interpretations will be placed upon this small work; for he that appears in print openly before all men, must not think it harsh to receive the retorting frowns of an enemy. It may well be free of offence, or at least of offending them. And as for myself, had I not learned to have borne such a burden, it would have been in vain to have taken a pen in my hand. For it is not written to any one particular person, but for everyone, and amidst the many imagined ways of worship, I am looked at awry by some, and in case my opponents should take a pen in hand with any other intent, it is probable they might be frustrated in their aims.

If I had looked for the applause of men, I might have enjoyed more in silence, than in revealing my mind, and laying myself open to the view of my enemies, if there are any such. But let all men conclude, if they expect any answer from me in that regard, they will be far mistaken in their intentions: for I have not so learned Christ, as to make Him my stalking horse, to carry my envy; but rather desire His assistance as an aid, to admonish all men. For love has so much of the nature of truth, that it will abolish all envy, pride, self-conceitedness and fear. So I would have all men to understand that I consider it below me, to take note of anyone's praise, or disapproval of this [text]; yet not below me to reveal what I have received, and to contend for the truth, and not to bind my talent up in a napkin. Lest I should neglect to do the will of my Master, and so be called to account for it: therefore I do not prize the censure of any, having such a freedom in my intention as to my writing, my humble and more edifying information.

As for what anyone is pleased to consider me, [either] a friend or enemy, I have this hope, that as I shall not be much moved by any displays in men, so likewise I shall endeavour to keep myself from deserving any envy from anyone. Knowing that truth may have many assaults, yet the fortress will survive; happy is he that is a soldier in this same conquest, great will be his reward above all the endowments of this life. He need not press after the enslaving rudiments of this life, to serve where he ought to be served, so as to make captive that noble grain of wheat, by any unseemly tares of man's inventions. But his delight is in a higher and brighter lustre far transcending any enjoyment in this life, or of this construction.

Though his time here in this his earthly Tabernacle, seem as it were a pilgrimage of distress to what others enjoy, yet when he looks homeward, he has more cause to rejoice than to mourn. For what pleasure can any man assure himself of in anything that decays, if he but casts his eye towards the Rock, out of which he was hewn? Suppose you should be made heir of all the promising delights the world could offer; yet if you do not improve them to the advantage of your LORD and Master, it would have been better for you not to know them. But if you use them rightly, you cannot assure yourself of any continuance with them; for you are not at your own disposal, but must give up your power to Him, from whom you borrowed your time since your birth.

Oh! Do not loose the substance for a few fading vanities, which are but dry husks, that can never satisfy any, though they have so many of them. It is the nature of them to breed desire, and not to quench it, nor to enrich your treasury of content that is but a pearl. But that must be received from the Bridegroom, when He comes to welcome His guests, and to adorn each of His friends with a crown of glory and immortality, and eternal life; which everyone shall receive that has the wedding garment on, when He shall appear in His glory to show us the heavenly mansions that He has prepared for us.

Therefore, let us use all our endeavours that we possibly can, to nourish the more noble seed. And let us beware we do not stifle it in its womb, but rather seek to cherish it by feeding upon moderation, so that its birth may be hastened, and its glory manifested. Then your pleasant pastures will be beautified with that incomparable Lily, even righteousness, so that it may produce the effectual crop of peace and holiness, without which, no man can see God. Let us not become only hearers of the word, but doers of it also; knowing that the time past may suffice us to walk as we have walked, in the vanity of our minds. Seeking to lay aside all such superfluities of naughtiness, that we may learn to receive the grafted word in meekness, that is able to save our souls; and not to spend our time enjoying the seeming delights of this world, but rather show yourselves to be such as seek the kingdom whose foundation is laid in truth and righteousness. Laying up our treasure, where neither moth nor canker can pollute, nor thieves break through to steal, that we aim at that mark which gives just cause for joy in the end; 'For where your treasure is, there will your heart be also' (Matthew 6.21).

We will only show ourselves to be friends of God by doing the will of God; and then our beauty will become perfect through His comeliness, and we shall receive an unction from the Holy One, whereby we may come to know all things, even the deep things of God. Persisting from one degree of righteousness to another, to treasure up for ourselves that hope that will purge out all uncleanness, causing us to walk more wisely. Mourn over Him whom we have pierced, that neither grave nor death may have any more than what was assigned to them from the beginning; that so we may joyfully and conqueringly sing, 'O death where is thy sting? O grave, where is thy victory?' (I Corinthians 15.55).

This is the conquest that we have gained if we love God, we shall not [lack] that spiritual food, because He loves us, and in this we shall know if we love Him or not. For he that loves God, keeps His commandments, and His commandments are not grievous to him.

Thus desiring that each reader of this common, yet loving work, would cleanse themselves of all envy, lest they attack my weak endeavours with an envious dart, and they overreach, rendering themselves unfit for their more expedient war, by inflicting any former grudge upon this treatise. I would advise anyone that has anything against me, to let me suffer for that cause in which they consider me guilty, than to defame anything here, which their conscience tells them, is true. Let them render what they please, I hope I shall have enough love to banish all thoughts of envy, that might encroach into my delightful treasury, out of which this small treatise has proceeded.

I know many may attack me for my common speech, but let them conclude, if I had as much leisure to indict as they may have to peruse each word, I might have corrected some expressions; but let no-one envy my mean instructions knowing that they might proceed from as effectual a fountain of fervency as if they had had the appearance of a clever intellect.

Let it suffice my superiors, that I have not hindered the building of the Temple intentionally, but rather endeavoured to lend them my helping hand, to hew one small stone fit for the Builder's use. And if I find that this may in any way further or hasten the work, I shall have great cause to rejoice; it will be an encouragement for me to persevere in my intended work. I entreat you not to despise its workmanship, knowing myself altogether unworthy to be employed in taking this work in hand; yet if my willingness stirs up the spirits of any who pursue this work, let them attribute the honour of it to the chief owner of the work, by whom I was both employed and instructed. If anything may prove advantageous to you, in this my invitation of love, repay it to my Instructor, and do not set up an image in your hearts to bestow anything of obedience to it. But sacrifice your whole heart to Him from whom you receive your life and being, that we may press forward towards the mark of the prize of the free calling of God, by giving to Him all the pre-eminence of what He has wrought for us.

And let us show ourselves to be His servants by planting the fruitful Vine of Love, so that our Lord's Vineyard may yield Him its proper fruits in due season. As He has demonstrated Himself to be God, and a Father to us: so we may give the strength of our minds, to serve Him in His commands, and then we shall receive the reward of good servants. This will be of more value to us, than all the delightsome husks of this life; which are at best transitory and changeable, as in respect of our more durable riches.

Though all the infrequent gusts of persecution

may meet us in our progress, in the several revolutions of this world, from which we may receive the loss of all other seeming pleasures, by those who oppose the truth; yet this will be our comfort, that we have treasure that no man can take from us. If we keep close to the truth, no-one can take away that treasure that is laid up for all those that shall be found conquerors, by the overcoming of the lusts and pride of this world in their exactness in the ways of truth. Their pleasure will be in desiring to be at their home and centre, knowing that there they shall take their rest. Whereas before they are dissolved from their earthly tabernacle, or house of this life, persecutions and afflictions are, or ought to be, as welcome guests as joy is expedient in that which is to come.

Herein is that ancient saying confirmed, that the way to heaven is through hellish persecution; therefore in your highest aspirations, let this be your aim, that God's pleasure may be yours, and take up your cross and follow Him; not valuing all the lets and impediments that may seek to hinder you from returning to your constant and abidable rest. Desire your beloved to make haste to take you in His arms, where you may sing unanimously, 'all praise be to Thee, O God'. And in the meantime desire your beloved to 'set me as a seal upon thine heart, as a seal upon thine arm: for love is strong as death; jealousy is cruel as the grave: the coals thereof are coals of fire, which hath a most vehement flame. Many waters cannot quench love, neither can the floods drown it: if a man would give all the substance of his house for love, it would utterly be contemned' (Song of Solomon 8.6,7).

This is the jewel that when a man has found, he sells all he has to purchase it, even the hidden Manna, that a man may eat, and satisfy himself with all. Which is food only for those that have the white stone given them, and a new name, written on it, that no man can read save he that receives it (Revelation 2.17). This is the new Commandment, even the old, even that which was from the beginning, love works no evil, neither renders evil for evil: but contrariwise good and forgiveness to his brother, even if he offend you seventy and seven times a day. This is perfect love that abhors slavery, by casting out fear, he that gets this pearl, ensures himself a safe hiding place, where the enemy cannot hurt him by rejoicing over him. For though he seems to fall, yet shall he arise, and the LORD will be a light to him. 'For his anger endureth but a moment; in his favour is life: weeping may endure for a night, but joy cometh in the morning' (Psalm 30.5).

Farewell,
Thomas Watson,
London, April 1661.

CHAPTER ONE

THE CAPTIVITY OF BABYLON

*For there they that carried us away captive
required of us a song; and they that wasted
us required of us mirth, saying, sing us one
of the songs of Zion. How shall we sing
the LORD's song in a strange land? If I
forget thee, O Jerusalem, let my right
hand forget her cunning. If I do not
remember thee, let my tongue cleave to
the roof of my mouth; if I prefer not
Jerusalem above my chief joy
(Psalm 137.3-6).*

The children of Israel in remembrance of their
captivity in general, recited this Psalm, as you
may read in the first and second verses. It
relates to their weeping and being oppressed
for the decay and wasting of Zion, and also
their awareness of their enemies' derision. But
in deriding them for their present sufferings,
and for their former mentioning of Zion, and
that their deliverance should be by the hand of
Him, who had been manifestly known to them

in times past, by the name of the God of Zion.

This text was Israel's recital, and it is, or may be any one man's or any peoples, that can by experience sympathize with these sad facts. I shall not seek to repeat any further the general discourse of this Psalm; but I shall in particular insist upon the words before mentioned in my text, in which I shall consider these five headings:

1. The People demanding.
2. The People [of whom it is] demanded.
3. The thing demanded.
4. Their answer to the demand.
5. The answer of God to them in the thing demanded.

1. The people demanding were the Babylonians or men of Babel; for so it is plainly understood in the first clause of the text, 'For there they carried us away captive'. If anyone were so scrupulous as to know where it is drawn from let him cast his eye to the first words of this Psalm, and he may find the answer himself. It was 'by the rivers of Babylon', or the rivers in Babylon; for there it was these prisoners of hope were carried.

2. The people demanded of were the Jews, as is suggested in verse 5: 'If I forget thee, O Jerusalem.'

3. The thing demanded is mirth, or one of the songs of Zion, as is plainly suggested in the last clause of the third verse, 'saying, sing us one of the songs of Zion'.

4. The peoples answer to the demand is plainly understood by these words, 'How shall we sing the LORD's song in a strange land?' Or, as some render it, 'How can we sing the LORD's song in a strange land?' judging it an impossibility to do so.

5. The answer of God to the Jews in the thing answered; this is plain in verse 4, 'How shall we sing the LORD's song in a strange land?' But mark the answer of God to these cast down and dejected Jews, in verses 5 and 6; 'If I forget thee, O Jerusalem, let my right hand forget her cunning. If I do not remember thee, let my tongue cleave to the roof of my mouth, if I prefer not Jerusalem above my chief joy.'

The doctrine in general will be this. That God's dearest and choicest people may be left in such a strait, that they may not know how to sing the LORD's song. I say, that those people whom God chiefly intends to make use of, to display Himself to in love and kindness, and set His name as a pillar in the midst of, may be driven to such a strait, that it seems impossible in their understanding to sing the LORD's song.

But before proceeding any further, let us consider these four particulars:

1. What this song of Zion signifies, or rather what is meant by 'the LORD's song?'

2. What it is that disables a people from singing this song of Zion.

3. In what land or state, this song of Zion may be said to be really, experimentally and truly sung.

4. By what means a people can be made capable or learned in this school, to sing the LORD's song.

CHAPTER TWO

THE SONG OF ZION

1.What this song of Zion signifies, or rather what is meant here by 'the Lord's song?'

What is the song of Zion, or what the enemies of the Jews might mean here by the demands of Israel? Zion is the city that God accepts for the improvement of all those that are of the flock of Abraham, and lineage of David; in that state where it is witnessed that Abraham was God's friend, and David a man after God's own heart. Therefore God gives this testimony of it, as He witnesses, that He would and did delight Himself in them; in Abraham and David. Even so, He witnesses that His dwelling is in Zion, and that, 'He hath desired it for his habitation' (Psalm 132.13). And as he has it in Psalm 76 'In Salem also is his tabernacle, and his dwelling place in Zion' (Psalm.76.2). And again in Psalm 84: 'They go from strength to strength, everyone of them in Zion appeareth before God' (Psalm 84.7). So the song of Zion arises from the occasion of God's dealing with His people in that dispensation, that He shows and reveals Himself to His people in.

But it is generally observed, that wherever there is any mention made of Israel singing of Zion's songs, there is mention made that the occasion of their song has relation to some conquest or other that they had gained. A conquest over moral enemies as men, or spiritual lustful wickedness in their hearts, in which they had experienced God's love in some way or other more than usual. But I suppose the song that these Babylonians required of them, was only that song sung to God at the time of their deliverance from the Egyptians, and other such enemies. Therefore I shall not speak of the former in this place, but shall defer until I open my text further. I shall chiefly insist upon this part, because it is most suitable to our purpose; for that song that was demanded of Israel, was such a hymn as required mirth, as their enemies understood mirth, not they thought that the Israelites would ever again be delivered out of their servitude, which they subjected them to by conquest.

This is plainly shown in Nehemiah 4, at the

beginning of the chapter, by Sanbalat and Tobiah the Ammonite, who stood and mocked them, saying, 'What do these feeble Jews? will they fortify themselves? will they sacrifice? will they make an end in a day? will they revive the stones out of the heaps of rubbish, which are burned?' (Nehemiah 4.2). Even saying, 'that which they build, if a fox go up, he shall even break down their stone wall.' The same enemies of Israel, as in this Psalm spoke these words (as you may read in 2 Chronicles 36.5-7). These were the people that were carried away captive in the time of Jeremiah, and as is mentioned by Ezra, 'that the word of the LORD by the mouth of Jeremiah might be fulfilled' (Ezra 1.1). I say, these are the people of whom a song is required.

Now let us search for what song Israel had sung to the God of Zion. If we turn to Exodus 15, we shall find what it is that Israel makes their mirth, and what is the occasion of their mirth or singing. Their being delivered from the hand of Pharaoh and the fury of the Egyptians chiefly occasioned the cause of their song. The song chiefly consists of prayers to their God, whom they owned to be their strength and salvation, and their deliverer. This is maintained through the whole song, and therefore I say the song of Zion that is here made mention of, is praises to their God, for their deliverance from their open and manifest enemies. In Deuteronomy 32, there we have Moses singing another song of the same nature as this, praising God for all His mercies in keeping and delivering His people; saying, it was the LORD alone that had delivered them, and that they had not in the least deserved it at His hands.

Again we have Deborah and Barak singing a similar song in Judges 5. In remembrance of what the LORD had done for Israel, in making use of so mean an instrument as a woman to take a king prisoner, it was God [they] said, that fought the battle, 'they fought from heaven; the stars in their courses fought against Sisera' (Judges 5.20). Thus, I say, the song of Israel, or the 'Hebrew song', as some translate it, or the song of Zion as is here spoken of, and demanded of the Jews, is praises to their God for their deliverance and ascribing to Him the honour. And now being taken and carried away captive by their enemies, they were deprived of the victory; and so their Babylonian deriders might justly laugh at them, and deride them for their captivity, saying 'sing us one of the songs of Zion', or praises to your God, for your deliverance from us. After God had given them into their hands as prisoners. But I will not assert that no more can be gleaned from these words, of a higher kind, but I suppose I may safely say that this was the song that was demanded. So I shall defer at this time to open its every particular clause, seeking to focus on the aspects presented, as God has given me ability. I shall scarcely touch each thing that I have intended.

2. What is it that disables a people from singing this song of Zion?

I shall be very brief in this place; I shall only give you three reasons, and then pass to my third point in the text.

The first and greatest debarment that a people can meet with, that may hinder a people from singing this song, is chiefly their sins. This I am sure, will hold with opening the text to the full scope of these words. I say that sin is the first stumbling block that occasions a people's inability to sing this song of being delivered from the hand of their enemies. This you have in the Lamentations of Jeremiah, 'Jerusalem hath grievously sinned; therefore she is removed; all that honoured her despise her' (Lamentations 1.8). This prophet was the messenger often sent, to bid and warn these people to return from their evil ways, as you may read in Jeremiah 36.20 to the end of the chapter. It is plainly declared that His love and zeal for Jerusalem is revealed; for though the king burned the roll which he presented, in defiance of his words, yet he is willing to write another at the command of the LORD, as he ever was to write the first. If it had been possible to have wrought any good upon them, he would not lack the means to intreat them to repent. But all was in vain as the people were altogether bent after their own willfulness, even from the king that sat upon the throne, to the priest that sat in the Temple. As the prophet sorely lamented 'thy prophets have seen vain and foolish things for thee: and they have not discovered thine iniquity, to turn away thy captivity; but have seen for thee false burdens and causes of banishment' (Lamentations 2.14).

It was a pleasing and melodious vision that these prophets saw for Israel, as indeed it is too frequent with most, if not all people, if they bend their minds to anyone's vanity. They choose to hear those prophesies which free them, as they think, from any guilt, if they should practice and follow such vanity. Therefore it was the opinion of an ancient heathen, that if any spoke well of his practices, he would ask him, what was required of him. For he supposed, that if any man spoke highly of him, it was to deceive him, that he might gain honour or reward by it; he thus had fervent affection for those that seemed to envy him, saying, he had none that instructed him more than his enemies. If they knew he offended, they reproached him for it, enabling him to know in part how far he offended in anything; I wish many Christians had a rule like this.

The fury of God is the next cause, which renders a people unable to sing this song. For as sin is the first cause, so God's fury is the effected cause of their inability. When God is moved by sin to afflict a people, after waiting a long time, it may be day after day, week after week, and year after year; yet He sees no hope of their return, and His fury is moved. It may be He will slay some by the sword, and give others to famine, and so He may revenge Himself of them for their high provocations, by which they have provoked Him to do it. So they shall know if His sword goes out against them in fury, it will not return void of effecting the cause of its being moved. So whilst God is taking vengeance upon a people, they cannot in any-wise be said to be sensible of singing this song; for the song praises God for deliverance, and no people can sing this song, unless the LORD be reconciled to them as a friend in love and peace.

The third thing, which hinders a people from singing this song, is the want of the Lord's presence in times of trial. For if love may be as great to them in times of trial as in peace, yet if it is not manifestly known to them to be so, they are very much disinclined to sing this song. It is recorded of Job, 'know that God hath overthrown me, and hath compassed me with his net. Behold, I cry out of wrong, but I am not heard: I cry aloud, but *there is* no judgement. He hath fenced up my way that I cannot pass, and he hath set darkness in my paths. He hath stripped me of my glory, and taken the crown from my head. He hath destroyed me on every side, and I am gone: and mine hope hath he removed like a tree' (Job 19.6-10). And as Solomon remarks elsewhere, 'oppression maketh a wise man mad' (Ecclesiastes 7.7).

I therefore say, that whoever does not see the face of the Lord to shine victoriously in his sight, cannot experimentally and knowingly sing this song. But he is as it were a stranger to the real and punctual harmony that the singers sing in. But I shall speak more fully of whom this song must be sung by in my following discourse [study].

CHAPTER THREE

WHERE THE SONG
OF ZION IS SUNG

3. In what land or state, this song of Zion may be said to be really, experimentally and truly sung.

For this we must first understand, that this song is the only song to be sung in the land of deliverance, and in this, it coherently answers the text, as it is opened. For it is not the place that hinders them from singing this song, but it is their want of God's power to assist them in any place, which makes the land seem strange for a people to sing this song. Israel could not account the wilderness a strange land, by reason they could sing it there, and though it was a strange land as Babylon, respecting their acquaintance with the place; but in respect of their participation in the love and favour of God, the land of Babel was stranger to them than the wilderness. In the wilderness they were delivered from their enemies, and in Babel their enemies restrained them from their liberty.

So they can only say they were restrained from singing this song, so long as they were prisoners; therefore they complained of the decays of Zion, because Zion was the city of their deliverance, and that being wasted, they were by that means made heirs of a strange land by being strangers to the song of Zion. This song cannot be sung outside of Zion, or the LORD's fortified city; therefore the prophet Zechariah says, 'And the LORD shall inherit Judah his portion in the holy land, and shall choose Jerusalem again' (Zechariah 2.12). The LORD is pleased to call Judah his portion, and He will inherit him in the Holy Land. Now there is no place that can be said to be unholy, as to what it is made at first, but by a people's pollutions of the land. This is seen in Psalm 102:19-20: 'For He hath looked down from the height of his sanctuary; from heaven did the LORD behold the earth. To hear the groaning of the prisoner; to loose those that are appointed to death.' For what purpose did He loose these prisoners? It follows in the next verse, 'To declare the name of the LORD in Zion, and his praise in Jerusalem'. This is also shown in Psalm 99: 'The LORD is great in Zion, and He is high above all people' (v.2).

This is as if the prophet should have said, the

inhabitants of Zion have set the praise of the LORD high above all people, or the praise of all people – Yes, even the LORD to reign in their hearts, and so it is in the last verse of Zechariah 2, 'Be silent, O all flesh, before the LORD: for He is raised up out of his holy habitation.' When the LORD is 'raised forth of his holy habitation', it is to conquer and subdue, and silence all flesh: then He himself may be in Zion, or Judah, or Jerusalem. Among the inhabitants of those places that are Jews indeed, and in action; not by being Jews, or sons of Zion by name, or profession only, for those are the true Jews, and sons of Abraham, that build up the decaying of Judah, and do the works of Abraham.

As the Apostle Paul says, 'wherefore henceforth know we no man after the flesh: yea, though we have known Christ after the flesh, yet now henceforth know we him no more' (2 Corinthians 5.16). And it is more plain in Romans: 'For he is not a Jew, which is one outwardly; neither is that circumcision, which is outward in the flesh: But he is a Jew, which is one inwardly; and circumcision is that of the heart, in the spirit, and not in the letter; whose praise is not of men, but of God' (2.28,29). As I said before, the people that willingly and joyfully do seek to repair the breaches of Judah, are such as must inherit the promises of God made to Abraham, Isaac and Jacob, and shall surely be inhabitants of this land, where this song of Zion may be really, and experimentally, and truly sung. But I shall leave this matter at this time, desiring that everyone who seeks to be an inhabitant of this land, to take note of what his duty must be in Zion, or in Judah: to which I shall speak more fully, when I come to show you the laws and ordinances that are in this land.

4. By what means a people can be made capable or learned in this school, to sing the LORD's song.

I shall endeavour through God's assistance to make clear before you the two following observations:

1. It chiefly concerns us to search who is the lawgiver in Zion, or who it is that instructs Jacob, or Israel.
2. What these laws or statutes are, that are taught or ought to be taught in Israel, and how these are observed.

1. Let us consider, that God is made mention of in several places to be the instructor of Israel, as in Psalm 78, 'He established a testimony in Jacob

and law in Israel' (v. 5). And in Isaiah: 'Thus saith the LORD, thy Redeemer, the Holy One of Israel; I am the LORD thy God which teacheth thee to profit, which leadeth thee by the way that thou shouldest go' (48.17). And again in Isaiah: 'Hearken unto me O my people, and give ear unto me O my Nation: for a law shall proceed from me, and I will make judge-ment to rest for a light of the people' (51.4). If anyone is not satisfied that it is spoken to Israel, the foregoing words will show this better, and as you have it again in Isaiah: 'O Zion, that bringest good tidings, get thee up into the high mountain; O Jerusalem that bringest good tidings, lift up thy voice with strength; lift it up, be not afraid; say unto the cities of Judah, Behold your God!' (40.4).

I might instance hundreds of places more to prove this truth to you; for wherever there is any mention made of the author of Israel's laws, and statutes, God is made mention of in some degree or other, to be the giver of them. If it is mentioned of Israel as Israel, or as I have defined Israel before, which is not so in name or show, but in truth and verity; it may be someone will demand of me, what is God?[1] This has often been an objection against

---

[1] This question is also dealt with briefly in the Westminster Assembly's *Shorter Catechism:* IV. *Question.* What is God? *Answer.* God is a spirit, infinite, eternal, and unchangeable, in his being, wisdom, power, holiness, justice, goodness, and truth.' (Ed)

me, but I shall speak very little to it in this place. First, God is said to be the 'Alpha and Omega', 'the first and the last' (Revelation 1.11). Secondly, God is said to 'feed his flock', and that He is their Shepherd (Isaiah 40.11). In other places He is revealed to be a 'God of fury to the wicked', it is one thing to look upon Him as He is himself, and another to look upon Him as He is in us, or in his manifestations, but I shall defer on this discourse, supposing that the unfolding of it may be a stumbling block rather than edifying to many.

Therefore, I shall advise everyone, to assure himself that there is no iniquity in Him, and that He is a hater of lies and a destroyer of all the works of the wicked. Thus I shall proceed to the second point. Showing what these laws or statutes are that which are given to Israel in Zion, or the Holy Land as some read it, or Judah, or in Jerusalem, and how these are to be observed.

2. Let us consider that as the Lawgiver is holy, so are His statutes and laws holy also. This is confirmed in the Psalms: 'Righteous art thou, O LORD, and upright are thy judgements. Thy testimonies that thou hast commanded are righteous and very faithful' (Psalm 119.137,138). And in verse 7 of the same Psalm: 'I will praise thee with uprightness of heart,

when I shall have learned thy righteous judgements.' So you plainly see that the statutes, laws and commandments of this Lawgiver to these inhabitants, is Righteousness, Truth, Equity, Love, and Faithfulness. And as you have a Righteous Lawgiver, and Righteous Laws, so you must serve Him in righteousness, if you intend to be a subject in this land. This is again seen in Psalm 118: 'Open to me the gates of righteousness: I will go into them, and I will praise the LORD: This gate of the LORD into which the righteous shall enter' (vv. 19,20)

You must not stand to frame a service to seek the bounty and gifts of men in it, but the Commands of God. Happy is that people that is brought to such uniformity, that it may be truly said of them, that the Statutes of the Lord are duly observed in their land.[2] But before proceeding further, let us consider what danger may ensue upon the inhabitants of this land, in case they do not obey and keep these Statutes and Laws.

First I say, that man as [a natural] man, is apt to deserve being cast out from inhabiting

---

[2] Watson neatly summarizes the puritan view of the role of the Law of God in the life of the Christian. It is the rule of the believer's life, and though he is justified by faith alone, in Christ alone, nonetheless he seeks to walk in the ways of righteousness. The obedience of faith is undoubtedly the main antidote to antinomianism. (Ed)

this land, but the Lawgiver is a God of Mercy as well as Justice. In case you are as strict an observer as may be, yet you cannot assure yourself of constant contentment in all things. For whilst you are in this decaying and frail house of this world, there will be turmoil and in the several revolutions and changes; whilst we are striving to conquer them by our high aspirations, the World, the Flesh and the Devil, will strive to show us their present seeming delights. Intermingling our more serious and reasonable undertakings with those things that have nothing but a show of godliness in them, and nothing of its power. This is the great warfare in which you must engage as a combatant, if you come into this land, for the flesh will be striving against the Spirit, and the Spirit against the flesh, and these two are contrary (Galatians 5.17). If you will seek any durable riches, any treasure that the moth and rust will not destroy, but it will abide all trials of this life, and will become purer each time it is cast into the fire; I say, if you seek to deal in such commodities, you must expect the frowns of your enemies. Indeed your King will be trying you, to see how your zeal agrees with your profession.

But lest you should think to escape this scourge or correcting hand of God, I will endeavour to show you that it is good to bear it, and continue steadfast to the end. Although there is a twofold affliction peculiar to the chiefly beloved of God, yet they shall receive a diadem at the last, that will cause them to acknowledge that it was good for them that they were afflicted.

First, there is an affliction that God suffers His children to be exercised with, as in respect of their having to do, or dealing with things of this life.

Secondly, there is an affliction as in respect of our dejections in things appertaining to our chiefest content, as when we are hindered in our commerce with God. When we lie sighing and complaining, as Job and several of his servants have done; Job says, 'Behold I go forward, but He is not there; and backward, but I cannot perceive Him' (Job 23.8). He would not appear to answer Job, in what Job desired, neither would He plead with him until his time was come, Job cried out of oppression (Job 19.7 & 23.3).

This is the heaviest burden of affliction, which may befall the children of God. It seems so burdensome sometimes, that they may be brought to question their condition to be worse than mere worldlings, who have no joy in anything else but what they grapple after in this life. David considered that it fared better with the wicked than the righteous, until he went into the sanctuary, then he realized it was better to draw near to God

(Psalm 73). How does God see them, say the wicked, though we scourge them? David says, that therefore are his people brought to that place, and water of a full cup is wrung out to them (Psalm 73.10).

CHAPTER FOUR

JERUSALEM AFFLICTED

Let no man mistake me, thinking that I speak of God's withdrawing His affection from His people. My meaning is only this, that God withdraws Himself in love to us, even as the apostle has it, 'every son whom I love, do I rebuke and chasten' (Hebrews 12.6). To keep our thoughts from the vanity to which all men are prone; to have high thoughts of their own strength, and their own ability, and their own righteousness. Or failing to search their own hearts, to acknowledge to whom we are obliged, forgetting the fountain out of which forgiveness flows and springs to us, as the apostle Paul says of the Romans, 'they have a zeal of God, but not according to knowledge' (Romans 10.2). As it is explained, 'they being ignorant of God's righteousness, and going about to establish their own righteousness, have not submitted themselves unto the righteousness of God' (Romans 10.3).

Even so, we are apt to conclude with

ourselves that we have this good qualification, or this good blessing, or I am so just or more righteous than such and such are. When we do consider if we are so, for it is God's mercy to us more than our deserving it, but rejoice in ourselves far above our sphere; not looking back to Him that gave it to us. For this, take one more scripture from the same apostle, 'But he that glorieth, let him glory in the LORD' (2 Corinthians 10.17).

Be sure of this, that whosoever receives any gift of grace, or any benefit to his spiritual refreshment, or any enjoyment to his souls happiness, or any blessing from the Lord, and does not attribute all the praise, glory and pre-eminence and honour to God that gave it to him, it would have been better that that man or woman had never received it. For he that forgets that God gave it to him, robs him of that praise and honour that is due to him, or gives himself the praise, or the praise of some other thing that is due to God alone.

So that which might through due obedience and thanks to God have been a blessing, may become a curse to him that misuses it. For 'to whom much is given, of him shall be much required' (Luke 12.48); and a servant shall be accounted an evil servant that hid his talent and safely restored it to its owner (Matthew 25.24-

26). What will he be accounted as that robs his Master and divides the talent, taking part of it for his own use, yet having the impudence to say, I have improved my talent better than such and such men? But it is well enough with him, and he has not been behind in giving his LORD what is due to Him. And if my man makes anything fit for his use, he will look to have the pre-eminence of it to himself, and yet he will not render the same to God.

Oh learn from the beasts of the field, and do not envy their service, unless you will act above pretence, 'The ox knoweth his owner, and the ass his master's crib: but Israel doth not know, my people doth not consider' (Isaiah 1.3). As you have it in Jeremiah, 'the stork in the heaven knoweth her appointed times; and the turtle and the crane and the swallow observe the time of their coming; but my people know not the judgement of the LORD' (8.7). And when the prophet Ezekiel was shown the transgressions of the people in his time, the LORD showed him that some worked abominations in the Temple of the LORD, as we read: 'And he brought me into the inner court of the LORD's house, and, behold, at the door of the temple of the LORD, between the porch and the altar, were about five and twenty men, with their backs toward the temple of the

LORD, and their faces toward the east; and they worshipped the sun toward the east' (Ezekiel 8.16).

By the east, as some translate it in this place, is meant those people looking for the chiefest light to consist in worshipping the Sun; this is a sad omen of the stirring or awakening of God's fury, when a people bend their minds to idolize any imaginary conceit of their own devising, bestowing the honour upon it, due only to God. He will have your whole heart, if He has anything of you, and in the right worship too; and not in any way we think is most rare because it is most harmonious in our sight. But in the exact way of the foregoing admonitions; even Christ, and His apostles, and the martyrs that were made to seal it with their blood, and not by praying to saints and martyrs, but to observe and do the things that they did. I mean the works that they did, and to praise God, in the same way as they did, and in the same thing. Let us seek to, 'press toward the mark for the prize of the high calling of God in Christ Jesus' (Philippians 3.14). Ascribing honour to whom honour is due.

I desire that you my beloved friend, indeed everyone to whom this treatise comes, that you seriously consider with your own hearts, how far you are behind with the LORD in this particular. This results from our unthankful-ness, that we have secured ourselves with, under the banner of forms and customary services, and we have not looked into the inside of things; to eat the kernel of the nut as well as gather the shell. As the nut cannot grow without the shell, so no man can experience the taste of the kernel by eating and feeding on nothing but the shell of the nut. God looks to the heart as well as to the tongue, therefore if you pray to God, check that your heart be joined to your tongue: that your tongue speak no more but the real symptoms of your heart, and that your heart be chiefly set on doing the will of God, and not on the beggarly elements of this world.

For if you follow the customs of others, framing any prayer as learned from a book and not by heart, you may justly think yourself far short of receiving any benefit by them from God. I do not say that is very good, take it in its place, for we cannot be servants of God without utterance and manifestation. This is my point, that no man [should] set a higher price on words, but consider the word is chiefly to yourself in your heart, and therefore make sure your heart be joined to your tongue, especially in prayer and praises to God. For if your prayers and praises to God are built on no more durable a rock than formal or customary uses, it will be in danger of being blown up by the encroaching gusts of covetousness and hopes of worldly honour, preferring the applause of men.

These will become upper[most] in you minds, so that you cause the more noble and excellent wheat to be choked by the tares in your more worthy land or vineyard. If you have no deeper root in religion than this, you will soon be brought to leave this upon any final occasion; for if one must be left, then, farewell profession, for I must leave you [to] embrace honour, and riches, and pleasures. I and the good words of men, you shall have the name so long as my better friends can have their entertainment; but if one must be left, then farewell prayer, and farewell praises, for I can pray as well in another dispensation, but I shall get nothing but the ill will of men, and the loss of honour and estate if I continue in this way. It was good and honourable, but now it is safe, I have had the company of my friends, wealth, honour and applause, but I must now follow them further, or else they will leave me. Oh, it is a sad thing, when religion, says God, is one thing today and contrary the next day, only for money and self-ends. This is one way of worshipping God, so called; but I fear it is no better than worshipping yourself, and in the worst sense too, for in this you toil to gather coals and faggots to consume yourself on the last day, without the great mercy of God.

In this manner of serving God, or rather yourself, it may be performed at any time, or in any sort of profession. But if you take up your rest in anything that is self-centred, know assuredly, that God will blast it in the end, if it is built on no surer ground than your own notions. It may be that God will let you alone for the time you will spend in this world, but your end will prove more bitter. The most wicked men may seem to have a rest, yes a pleasant one to their minds and desires it may be, but it is not lasting; it does not abide, as the prophet says, 'there is no peace, saith the LORD, unto the wicked' (Isaiah 48.22).

That is, no abiding or continuing peace. Therefore, value your future peace beyond any seeming present content in this life; for you must give an exact account of all your actions in the end. Remember what Solomon says:

'Rejoice, O young man, in thy youth; and let thy heart cheer thee in the days of thy youth, and walk in the ways of thine heart, and in the sight of thine eyes: but know thou, that for all these things God will bring thee into judgement. Therefore remove sorrow from thy heart, and put evil away from thy flesh: for childhood and youth are vanity' (Ecclesiastes 11.9-10).

Therefore I say, look well, yes narrowly to your ways, lest you think to build a Tabernacle to entertain the Holy Spirit in your professions, you deceive yourselves, building an altar to sacrifice to the Prince of Darkness, to your souls ruin, and eternal torment.

But to show you more plainly the description of the afflictions that God's dearest children are liable to in this life, I shall give you a brief introduction. It is my intention to speak more fully to the duty of Christian life, and how to bear the affliction and trying scourge of God's chastisements. But before proceeding further, let me lay this down as an undeniable maxim, that God never tries a nation or a people generally with trials which deliver them into the hands of their enemies, unless it be for their sins. But the trials that I intend to discuss, are such, which the children of God are liable to in particular when their Father withdraws His presence from them. In respect of showing them what He has done for them, though His love may be as great for them at this time as ever; such are struck at and overturned in their expectations. I have never read of God hiding Himself from any so long, that before the time was over, they found it was not in vain to serve Him, but appears in one or another to prove Himself a loving and tender God. Solomon says this, speaking of God withdrawing Himself from the church, for their high thoughts of their own righteousness, 'I have put off my coat, how shall I put it on? I have washed my feet; how shall I defile them?' (Song of Solomon 5.3).

She thought herself secure enough, and clean enough, yes, too clean to entertain her Beloved, though He told her, 'my head is filled with dew, and my locks with the drops of the night' (Song of Solomon 5.2). So His calls were too dark for her to understand, although His voice seemed to be like the voice of her Beloved, yet she could not think on the drops of the night that hung upon His locks; she was too clean to entertain Him. But Christ had 'put his hand by the hole of the door' (Song of Solomon 5.4), then her heart was moved for Him, and her hands 'dropped myrrh'. As soon as Christ put His hands into the holes of the door, she desired to have more of Him, but when she opened the door, she found, 'my beloved had withdrawn himself, and was gone', and would not appear to her through that door. She acknowledged that her soul failed when He spoke, which is as much as if she should think that this providence was not efficacious to her, in which she thought herself too clean. And so her soul failed her or her confidence, and she sought Him, but could not find Him, and called for Him, but He gave no answer. She now seemed lost, though she thought herself to be too clean.

The watchman found her as they walked about the streets, and they smote her and wounded her and the keepers of the wall took away her veil from her. This is the greatest trial that can in any way befall the church of God, to lack the presence of God to answer them in their afflictions. Indeed it is more than the absence of God, or His not appearing to answer them in what they think to find Him in, causing this affliction to be so great. As the church did [not] perceive that she had any need of such a guest as Christ, seeing as He did not appear in that cleanness in which she thought herself blessed. But when she felt the pleasant odour that proceeded from Him, and, charges the daughters of Jerusalem, 'if ye find my Beloved, that ye tell Him, that I am sick of love' (Song of Solomon 5.8).

When she had experienced the smell that He left behind, then she could not be satisfied without Him. And she does not search for Him in Babylon, or hear tidings of Him in Egypt or Edom; but of the daughters of Jerusalem. There it was that she found Him examining, 'What is thy Beloved, more than another beloved?' (Song of Solomon 5.9). As you have her demonstrating of Him in verse 10, to the end of the chapter. When she has given Him as magnificent praise as she could manifest, then she sums it all up in one word, 'He is altogether lovely'.

But before Christ appeared to manifest Himself to His church, to open their eyes, they were laid down to sleep securely; supposing themselves righteous enough, and clean enough, and pure enough in that which she had received. Look well to yourselves, all you that profess yourselves to be actors upon the stage of religion, that you do not entertain this guest of self-conceitedness, and so shut Christ out of doors. For this church had not long before had as high a sight, and as sensible an understanding as any that ever I read of in the Old Testament. This is clear in the second chapter of the Song of Solomon, 'I charge you, O ye daughters of Jerusalem, by the roes, and by the hinds of the field, that ye stir not up, nor awake my Love, till he please' (Song of Solomon 2.7).

Yet now He is awake, she still will not open the door to Him, nor give Him any entertainment, and all is occasioned by His locks being filled with the drops of the night. But when He had shaken them off, then she comes to find the same truth again to feed on. You shall plainly find how she is enabled to let Him take his repose, 'His left hand should be under my head, and his right hand should embrace me' (Song of Solomon 8.3). These words are mysteriously spoken, for the left hand of God is seldom used to administer His embraces to the people of the church of God, unless it be such embraces as He bestows upon them when His locks are filled with the drops of the night; for God most gloriously unveils our mind with the strength of His right hand, when He has laid His left hand under His head; then He shall not be awoken, till He please. Oh! It is one of the fullest sayings in the whole scriptures, it is as much as saying; 'not my will, but thy will be done, O God' (Matthew 26:39).

Yet for this church not to know her Beloved, is a sad and sudden alteration, as the prophet Jeremiah has something of this nature concerning the daughters of Zion: 'For I have heard a voice as a woman in travail, and the anguish as of her that bringeth forth her first child, the voice of the daughter of Zion, that bewaileth herself, that spreadeth her hands, saying, Woe is me now! For my soul is wearied because of murderers' (Jeremiah 4.31).

Oh Zion, Zion! What need is there for you to fear the LORD is exalted in you; yes, He has chosen to dwell with you, and to be lifted up in you. He has set the two pillars of His name in the midst of you; yes, what greater pillars are there to manifest His Name upon the earth, than Wisdom and Knowledge, and them to give this character of Him, 'The fear of the LORD is his treasure.'[1] Oh! What stronger fortress can you have Zion, than the fear of the LORD, than the love of your God? For thus it is here shown, that this is not a slavish fear, nor a dreadful or terrifying fear; no, this is such a fear that is here mentioned, for it may well be compared to what the Apostle calls love, which casts out slavish fears (1 John 4.17). And God promises further to be her security, 'not one of the stakes thereof shall ever be removed, neither shall any of the cords thereof be broken' (Isaiah 33.20).

And He will not only be her safety to keep her secure, but [also] He will take vengeance on her enemies also, and plead her controversy with those that rise up against her; surely, anyone might think that Zion would sleep so securely. But here Zion spreads out her hands crying, 'Woe is me now! For my soul is wearied because of murderers' (Jeremiah 4.31). As if she says, my Comforter has left me, my Beloved is gone, my joy is turned into bitter-ness,

[1] Isaiah 33:6; Ed.

my melody into sadness, [and] my mirth into sighing and sobbing. This she expresses more plainly, 'The LORD hath forsaken me, and my God hath forgotten me' (Isaiah 49.14). When the prophet was proclaiming her deliverance, and the opening of her eyes, as you may read in the following verses, 'can a woman forget her suckling child, that she should not have compassion on the son of her womb?' No, then He shows her, 'I have graven thee on the palms of my hands.' He bids her to consider the matter.

So as I said before, the church of God and the people whom He loves, with an unmeasure-able and ever abiding love, may be at such a loss, that often they may think the LORD has withdrawn His affection clean from them. But I seldom find that He does not stay their hearts that they trust in Him, that their deliverance must be through Him. Though many times He tries their fidelity and zeal to Him and His Name, and at other times He afflicts them for backsliding and careless walking.

This brings them to walk worthy of such a God, who has laid up such good things in store for them. I might speak a great deal more on this manner of God dealing with His peculiar people in this life. But I shall forbear speaking any more of this, till we speak of them, namely the children of God; yes, those that are dear to him, jointly in their duty.

There is a second affliction peculiar to these beloved ones. Whereas you have them conquered, as it were, you now have them as conquerors and champions. For the Captain of their salvation bids them go on and fear not, so that, 'neither death, nor life, nor angels, nor principalities, nor powers, nor things present, nor things to come, nor height, nor depth, nor any other creature, shall be able to separate us from the love of God, which is in Christ Jesus our LORD' (Romans 8.38,39).

Now here you have the Shepherd leading out His sheep into pleasant pastures of content-ment, and now they know His voice so well, that they will not give ear to strangers. Though they are tempted with all the seeming delights of strangers, with rich rewards according to appearance, with promises of preferments, with all their enchantments; yet all these will not tempt them from those fruitful pastures, for nothing can allure them from this contented meadow, where they have the presence of their delightful Shepherd, giving them their meat in due season. So that stolen waters are not sweet to them, nor bread eaten in secret (Proverbs 9.17).

They know that the associates and reporters of such things shall have their portion with unbelievers, in a degree far remote from their rest, or contentment. For their delight is in the law of the LORD their God (Psalm 1.2), to show His praise and His glory in working wonder-fully amongst the sons of men. And to declare to others what God has done for them, and for the welfare of their souls, 'thou shalt forget the share of thy youth, and shalt not remember the reproach of thy widowhood any more. For thy Maker is thy Husband; the LORD of Hosts is his name; and thy Redeemer the Holy One of Israel; the God of the whole earth shall He be called' (Isaiah 54.4,5).

He bids them 'Awake, awake; put on thy strength, O Zion, put on thy beautiful garments, O Jerusalem, the holy city: for henceforth there shall no more come into thee the uncircumcised and the unclean. Shake thyself from the dust; arise, and sit down, O Jerusalem: loose thyself from the bands of thy neck, O captive daughter of Zion' (Isaiah 52.1,2). So that by arising from the dust and sitting still, the LORD will redeem you from all your captivities that have occasioned you distress, causing you to howl and weep. You shall be delivered from all your burdens that you have unjustly borne, for He has taken it upon Himself to plead the controversy of His people. So now they need not fear what befalls their bodies, for they have sufficient contentment, that it shall be well with their soul, they 'fear Him, which after He hath killed hath power to cast into hell' (Luke 12.5).

Though the world rages against them, and their neighbours envy them, and their kindred, and the dearest relations here below mock and scoff; is it any more than the Captain of your salvation endured for you through His suffer-ings? Do you not know that if you will be His disciples, then you must wear your Master's livery?[2] Yes, though it is dyed with a deep crimson as His was on the cross, it is not sufficient that servant is made equal with his Master? (John 15.20).

I am sure that any earthly servant would consider it a great honour, if he were permitted to wear a garment made of the same piece of cloth as his master wears. Even so, will all these that have experienced the honour and reward that is laid up at the end of their journey, for no man can prevent them receiving it.

Therefore I say these are not at all amazed at these things; no, they are no more than the honourable garments that all the guests of the Bridegroom must put on. And that with much willingness too, if it is laid down for you or offered to you; surely there is no man who would rather choose a diamond than a cornelian,[3] if he

[2] In the Middle Ages a man wearing the livery, the cloth or badge of his earthly lord, would show that he is retained in the service of one greater than himself. It was worn publicly as a symbol of service and honour. (Ed)

[3] Or a piece of quartz. (Ed)

knows the worth of each. Even so, will all those that have experienced the love of Christ Jesus, and the contentment that is in His ways; and the reward that shall be received by owning Him in truth and righteousness upon the face of the earth, in the presence of His foes. They will show themselves to be children of their Father, and servants of their Master. These stewards will know their Master is not only able, but willing to give to those that will labour in His vineyard, of the abundance of its pleasant fruit. They will also tell others what a loving and tender God He has been to them, and what contentment is to be had in obeying Him, and what safety there is in His paths, 'Her ways are ways of pleasantness, and all her paths are peace' (Proverbs 3.17).

Surely the way of the LORD is great pleasure to them that know the plainness, evenness, and exactness of it aright. To them there is great pleasure in walking in His ways; but the slothful cry out, there is a lion in the way (Proverbs 22.13). Therefore he will not venture, but lie down and take his ease, folding his eyes a little more in sleep, or in his dark rest. He would rather put up hazards, as man used to say, than encounter this lion that will bereave him of all his lustful desires, and all his worldly pleasures. Heaping together the unrighteous

Mammon of this world, by defrauding the simple, and usurping the just privileges of the poor, the innocent, and the harmless. But there is one other point, for there is a Bear that he must meet, which at best will scare him, if not tear him in pieces and devour him.

Whereas those that have been exercised in a manner of walking in this way, enjoying the pleasant sunshine of God's most glorious and unfathomable love; they know after the darkest night, the morning will produce light again, and dispel the darkness. So they never see so dark a cloud as God's fury in their way, yet it shall not be a Bear to them. No, they know the Sun will break through, if they keep constant in this way, and do not go astray from its punctual rules.

It is not a prison or a dungeon that will scare them, nor any earthly power that is contrary to the truth. They know that if the powers of men do not stand according to the truth of God, I say, their lives will not be dear to them, so dear that [they] would not rather part with their lives, than the portion of truth they have received. Calling light darkness, and darkness light; dis-honouring Him whom they know is able to keep them safe in the most evil and worst of days.

Look well to this, every man and woman, and lay not any burden upon each other, by unjust and unrighteous walking. For this is the end of a Christian: that God shall have no dishonour by his walking. If you deny God in this, pray that He does not deny you before the Angels in Heaven.

CHAPTER FIVE

THE CHRISTIANS DUTY OF OBEDIENCE TO CHRIST

i) Charity

Before we proceed further, let us consider what observation we ought to make of the performance of these holy laws. As I have shown, in the previously mentioned laws, you must observe that as the Law-giver is Holy, Just and Good; so are His Laws, Righteousness, Peace, Love, Faith, Truth, Patience, Equity, Justice, and Forgiveness. Whoever does not observe and fulfill these laws, will be liable of being cast out of this land, and from participating in the benevolence and fruition of this Law-giver.

Therefore, let us walk wisely in our station, for the short time that we are able to live in this frail house, that when we come to give an account of all our actions, we may approach His throne with all boldness. Laying hold upon Him who is our Righteousness, Peace,

Sanctification and Redemption. Knowing nothing of evil by ourselves, yet knowing nothing of Justification in our works or by our works, as proceeding from them. There is no-one that is an inhabitant of Zion but must observe and do the will of Him that is the Law-giver. These are the duties of the subjects in this land, which when Israel discerned they had broken and that it was their disregarding the statutes and laws of Zion, that occasioned their imprisonment; this is now considered as causing their grief, and on such a scale that it bursts out.

In order that all the captives that are in this captivity, respecting their inward freedom, may know how to release themselves, let them observe and keep the following invitations. In case they have broken these laws, they may mourn and mend their ways by walking more wisely, and so be delivered. Repent and mend your ways, take my advice and press forward.

First, we will show what these laws are, that you may know how to keep them. The first and greatest commandment is, 'Thou shalt love the LORD thy God with all thy heart, and with all thy soul, and with all thy mind, and with all thy strength'; the second is, 'Thou shalt love thy neighbour as thyself' (Mark 12.30,31). Not that they differ, but hold all in one; for you cannot honour God more in any one thing, than by loving your poor neighbour. It is the poor sons of God, if I may say, that have need of your charity, and not He that is creator of all things. For Christ says plainly to those on His right hand, 'For I was an hungered, and ye gave me meat; I was thirsty, and ye gave me drink: I was a stranger and ye took me in: Naked and ye clothed me: I was sick, and ye visited me: I was in prison and ye came unto me.... Inasmuch as ye have done it unto the least of these my brothers, ye have done it unto me' (Matthew 25.35,36,40).

If you have a mind to praise God on earth, or while you live here, deal justly with all men, and as near as possible you can make it your aim, to deal the same bread to others as you would have God deal to you. Fear that your heart should deceive you, in doing to others as you would have them do to you. I say, that this is a rule of rules, if truly observed, but beware of your heart deceiving you in this, and you think you do it, when you fall far short of it and so deceive yourself.

For I consider it the one and only way to show God's praise, to deal faithfully with all men in all things; especially to them that are without or of another mind, for you may gain him to do likewise. Whereas if you do the contrary, he would not only be emboldened, but would defame and reproach your way of worship, bringing scandal on all others walking in the same profession. And not only this, but dishonour would be brought on the Name of your God also; I desire all professors not to be weary in this respect, lest the heathen condemn us in that great day of trial. Do not enquire of the evil of your days, but take the Psalmist's direction – 'What man is he that desireth life, and loveth many days, that he may see good? Keep thy tongue from evil, and thy lips from speaking guile' (Psalm 34.12,13).

And it is beneficial for us, to speak and act the truth, so as I said before, it is the only way to show God's praise. As for what is done in private, it is done only upon account of our souls, it is a conference between God and us, concerning our souls' welfare. But what we do before men either shows the praise or dishonour of God. As Christ says, 'Take heed that you do not your alms before men, to be seen of them' (Matthew 6.1); He does not command you to hold up your charity before men, but not to give only because men see it, we must not make it our chief end. If we give to be praised of men, we have our reward; if we give before thousands, and could as freely give if there was no man [standing] by, giving it only to nourish their bodies: knowing we are [merely] stewards of it, and our Master may take it away from us when He pleases. For it is given for this intent, to feed the hungry and clothe the naked. Administering to the necessities of such as are in distress, and in such cases it ought to be as really theirs as ours, for we are but stewards of it.

If the LORD finds that we do not distribute faithfully according to His will, He can take it out of our hands in a moment, calling us to account of our stewardship. But mark what the Apostle John says, 'But whoso hath this world's good, and seeth his brother hath need, and shutteth up his bowels of compassion from him, how dwelleth the love of God in him?' (1 John 3.17).

Not that I conclude that the love of God must be in every man that relieves the needy, but be sure that these are manifestations of God in His people. Some will relieve the poor, because their fathers have done so before them, and so they will not have their name decay, but will seek to uphold it amongst men.

Others it may be, will give to the poor, because they will exceed such and such men that have as great estates as they, to give their praise. But alas! all this does not reach the mark of a Christian, for you may give all your goods to the poor or your body to be burned, 'and have not charity' it profits you nothing (1 Corinthians 13.3). And the widow's mite (Mark 12.43,44) is more than all this, which is as little as may be. If you cast your gift into this treasury with any acceptance, do not stay yourselves on this, as a sure foundation. It is not enough to give, but you must give with all your heart, yes, even, as to the LORD, knowing it is one of the greatest precedents of Christian verification.

As you must be willing and cheerful, so you must be careful too in your alms; you must not do it as if you did not care how or when you did it. Nor as many do nowadays, it is to be feared, they do the work of the LORD, negligently: religion is too commonly looked upon with too careless an eye, only for outward show and ceremonial traditions.

I say, you must study to do good works; yes, how you do them, that you glorify God in doing them, advancing His interest, and magnifying His Name. That He may have the pre-eminence of all, and therefore Christ bids them, 'But when thou doest alms, let not thy left hand know what thy right hand doeth' (Matthew 6.3). So it seems there is a left hand that is contrary to the right, that is prying into your alms giving. It is such a left hand that is apt to declare your doing to be praised of men; therefore Christ bids us to take heed, as in the next verse He plainly intimates, 'that thine alms may be in secret, and thy Father which seeth in secret himself shall reward thee openly' (Matthew 6.4).

This left hand is a member of that body which you have mentioned of the right hand in the previous chapter, 'And if thy right hand offend thee, cut it off' (Matthew 5.30). Lest it should occasion the whole body being cast into Hell. I wish we did not have too many such hands in our profession, in these times, that would rather administer to our applause in religion before men, than to glorify God, or relieving others that are in distress.

I ask earnestly, that you look well into your hearts, and examine them thoroughly, that you repent of any such thing 'while it is day' (John 9:4). For God will find you out in the end: therefore, be careful in your deeds of charity, if you intend to glorify God, or reap any benefit to yourselves. Do it with 'a pure heart, and of a good conscience, and of faith unfeigned',[1] as Paul charged Timothy. So everyone must make it his duty to be careful in this, lest you deceive yourselves, waiting for a reward, which you have already from men; from whom you sought it in parting with your gift. I must confess, in this area

[1] I Timothy 1:5; Ed.

91

you may come very near to the mark in your own view, feeding the hungry and clothing the naked and relieving the oppressed. That is a very good work, if done to a good end. But how can you say you do it to any good end, or aim at God's glory, when you set yourself in the highest degree in your alms, respecting your own praise, that men should adore you for it?

No, do not mistake yourself, for 'no man can serve two Masters', for he will neglect one or the other. God will either have all your service, or He will not accept any. He will have no partners, but as He created and formed all things, so He will have the pre-eminence in all things; both by you and all others, either to your eternal happiness, or else by showing His power on you to your destruction. Therefore resolve to be careful, if you expect the praise of God, or have any love of His Name, to do His work willingly and zealously; and be wary that the devil does not deceive you in any one thing, so taking away its efficacy from you by any of his cunning wiles. For he will watch all opportunities to ensnare you in your charity, knowing it to be one of the great pillars of a believers warfare.

As you must be willing to give your alms, and be careful how you give them, so you must be ready to give them. For if you say that you are willing to relieve any in distress, yet when your conscience tells you, that such and such poor people are in distress, and you do not relieve them, as the Apostle has it, 'Do all things with all readiness.' And 'For I know the forwardness of your mind, for which I boast of you to them of Macedonia, that Achaia was ready a year ago; and your zeal hath provoked very many' (2 Corinthians 9.2). The Apostle makes his boast of their readiness to administer to the necessity of such as were in distress. Yes, he urged it on others, that they may walk by his example, as not knowing any[thing] of more use in this life, it being one of the most needful models of a Christian, as Paul says, 'your zeal hath provoked very many.' Therefore I say, as you profess to have received the love of God, so let your love abound towards your brethren, as Christ says, 'Let your light so shine before men, that they may see your good works, and glorify your Father which is in heaven' (Matthew 5.16).

God is the Father of such love, and He will not be ashamed to own these that do this work willingly and carefully; for in this we represent Him, for He blesses us freely of His own willingness, as it is expressed, 'of his own will begat He us with the word of truth' (James 1.18), and

[as] He is careful of us, so will we not be careful to serve Him? As you have it in the Psalms, 'Behold, He that keepeth Israel shall neither slumber nor sleep' (Psalm 121.4). He is ready to shower His blessings and mercies on us, for 'He knoweth what things ye have need of' (Matthew 6.8); as if He studied to know our wants, and keeps those things for when we have need of them; 'For everyone that asketh receiveth; and he that seeketh findeth; and to him that knocketh it shall be opened' (Matthew 7.8). So if you will but go to the Fountain, that you may drink freely, it is not locked from you; unless you bring a poisoned pitcher with you, to destroy yourselves and defame the Fountain. I hope you will acknowledge His love to be as great in this as in anything; surely men would be careful and ready to serve such a God who is good to them, if they regarded their own welfare. I wish you could experience the Apostle's words in this one area, although he was speaking of another when he said, 'for the love of Christ constraineth us' (2 Corinthians 5.14).

Surely anyone that professes himself to have received more than others, he will show this in the sight of others, on every or many occasions. I do not say this, to keep any from striving, to walk in the highest manner that may be; but knowing that the dearest of God's people may be overtaken in a fault. None can bypass this fault without great remorse and grief of heart for it, and they could willingly redeem the time if possible, by a private repentance, or public instruction to others. But this is a style too high to speak of in these times I fear, yet assure yourselves, it is no more than ought to be in every professing Christian: for if you seriously consider your own hearts, you will find it is not a careless thing to profess Christ, and acknowledge yourselves His servants, you must expect to do His will. If you will be approved worthy of such a Master, as I shall show you more clearly afterwards.

As you must be willing to give charity, and careful in how you do it, being ready to give, so you must be bountiful and liberal. In your charity you must not lay up corrupt treasures, to buy a Lordship, or even a small cottage, neither if you see your poor brethren are in need. It was an excellent observation of a late deceased scholar, who when the officers of the parish came to him for money, they argued the needfulness of men's bounty in such a good work, saying, there was nothing of more concern than repairing the Temple of the LORD; he answered saying, it was needful and justifiable before God and man, but he warned them not to mistake the dead temple for the living temples, and so fail in their intent in both.

So I would encourage all those that profess themselves religious in their actions, in obedience to God's will, that they do not mistake themselves, adorning the dead temple with superfluous variety, when the living temples lack the necessities to keep themselves alive, look well to yourselves. I account it my duty to deal plainly with you, I fear it is too common in our day. For the love I bear toward you in Christ Jesus, I could wish it were otherwise with many of you; for if you neglect repairing the living temples, there is nothing that will hold in any harmonious tune in religious obedience. It is not enough to say, "the Temple of the LORD, the Temple of the LORD", you must show yourselves to mind the Temple of the LORD. It is not a feigned profession nor a guilded ceremony that will serve your turn, nor mine on the Last Day; but as we profess to have received more than others, let us walk more righteously and faith-fully than they do. That we may not condemn them with our tongues, and condemn ourselves in our actions in the sight of God and men.

For we may seem before men to be zealous for the LORD, and we may think that we are so; but mark what Solomon says, 'There is a way that seemeth right unto a man, but the end thereof are the ways of death' (Proverbs 14.12).

And Isaiah says, 'To what purpose is the multitude of your sacrifices to me? saith the LORD: I am full of the burnt offerings of rams, and the fat of fed beasts' (Isaiah 1.11). God would not have so much of these ceremonies but the effects of them; that is, 'cease to do evil. Learn to do well; seek judgement, relieve the oppressed, judge the fatherless, plead for the widow. Come now, and let us reason together, saith the LORD: though your sins be as scarlet, they shall be as white as snow; though they be red like crimson, they shall be as wool' (Isaiah 1.16-18).

If we bring these sacrifices before the Lord, He accepts them, and will delight Himself in us. But should we forget to bring these with us, we had better stay away, than come before God in vain; to expect a blessing when there is none assigned for us. It is to as much purpose for a man to think he has true faith in Christ, when he has not charity, as it is for a builder who seeks to build a tower, when he has only one stone to build it with. Remember what James says of such, 'For as the body without the spirit is dead, so faith without works is dead also' (James 2.26).

True, you may have faith to believe there is a God, even so did Pharoah, King of Egypt, 'The LORD is Righteous' (Exodus 9.27). Yet, he would not obey Him, nor leave the worshipping of idols,

til the LORD overthrew him and his host in the midst
of the sea. You may also read of Nebuchadnezzar
in Daniel 3. Although he believed that Daniel's
God, was LORD of kings, he set up an image
contrary to what Daniel worshipped. So as I said
before, it is not enough to have a faith; you must
have a working faith, a living faith, a steadfast faith,
and an upright and charitable faith. As Paul says:
'He which soweth sparingly, shall also reap
sparingly; and he which soweth bountifully shall
reap bountifully. Every man according as he
purposeth in his heart, so let him give; not
grudgingly, or of necessity: for God loveth a
cheerful giver' (2 Corinthians 9.6,7).

Not that God is not able to provide a sufficient
satisfaction for His children without your help. But
know this, He will try you, O man. How far your
charity will extend toward your weak and helpless
brother; God does not make use of us for His
need, but for His pleasure that He takes in seeing
us improve our talents. And that we should show
to all the world, that we are a people that have a
God who exceeds all other gods, in love,
tenderness, bounty and strength. How would all
people stand reviling our God, and disdaining our
way of worship, if they should see us walk loosely?
They would be apt to say, 'look how profane and
vain a thing it is for such and such men, who profess

they walk in a higher and more clear light than we do; but they let their brethren lack bread and clothes and can wear such needless trifles, and build such grand houses that we can content ourselves without.' I say, these things may be done, see that you leave the less needful undone. Know that the life of your poor brother is as precious in the sight of God, as your own. Your vain manner gives your enemies cause to revile you, and defame your brethren, and blaspheme the worthy Name of our God. Whereas, by walking more strictly, wisely and charitably, the mouths of all such people will be stopped.

They will be ready to commend your way of worship, and to praise those with whom you associate yourselves, and to glorify the Name of God, 'by which you are called'. If you profess yourselves servants of God, you must walk in the ways of godliness; do not think it your duty, but your business to distribute your charity to all in distress and want. For you shall receive a recompense worthy of your labour. For if God 'spared not his only Son, but delivered Him up for us all' (Romans 8.32), surely you will not think too much of yourself, to serve Him in your estate, or rather His own. You will be found an unjust steward to let your Master's servants die for want of food, when

He has provided enough for them. Certainly, you would rather walk up and down from one end of the vineyard to the other, to see that all your fellow servants have their meat in due season, if you respect the love of your Master. And the praise of it will redound so far to you in the end, if you will perform His will, for He will make you one of His family for ever, and you shall reign in joy and gladness to eternity.

ii) Warfare

Now he that does this work of charity, must avoid having more respect for himself than for God in his heart. For the Devil will never stop searching to find out one tradition or custom of the setting up of self. He will seek some device or other, if you take this work in hand, to represent you as unstable in all your undertakings in one respect or other; knowing it to be one of the greatest fortresses for a Christian to acquire for his residence, if truly built. For without this uniformity it is impossible to put on the whole Armour of God, and not take up this with it. How can it be said you have armed yourselves with the Truth, when you have not obeyed the God of Truth? Or how can any man say that Righteousness is his breast-plate, when he neglects his Master's business and has left his Master's commands unobeyed? Indeed, how can any man say that his feet are 'shod with the preparation of the Gospel' (Ephesians 6:15), when he walks in obscure and dark ways?

If you have your feet shod with the Gospel, you will walk in the paths and the ways of the Gospel. Now Christ is the True and Righteous way, described in the Gospel, and He thought it not too much to sacrifice His life for us; you cannot have greater love, than to give up your life in obedience to God through Christ.

And as for your taking Faith as your shield, when you go to withstand the devil, you will be overcome if you fail to take Love with you. For the Devil will quickly spot a target to fire at, if you leave charity behind; for this take what the Apostle says, 'I will show you my faith by my works' (James 2.18). Then you may put on the Helmet of Salvation and the Sword of the Spirit, for 'as He which hath called you is holy, so be ye holy in all manner of conversation' (1 Peter 1.15). And elsewhere. 'hereby shall all men know that ye are my disciples, if you love one another' (John 13.35). In Galatians, the fruits of the Spirit are, 'love, joy, peace, long-suffering, gentleness, goodness, faith, meekness, temperance' (Galatians 5.22).

It is vain to think of withstanding the Devil, for he will wound in one respect or another, if you do not put on all your armour, even the whole Armour of God (Ephesians 6:11).

He that undergoes this duel, or makes war against this enemy needs to be very studious to know what it is that he is to encounter. For your enemy goes about daily seeking to circumvent you. So when you make war against lying and deceit, beware he does not overcome you, but imputing strength to yourself in your striving, and so get into your harbour, weakening your strength and fort. Likewise when you fortify yourself against unrighteousness, he will present you with a seeming righteousness, that if you are not very watchful, shall give you more content than any you have chosen, if you do not know experimentally the odour that is in your choice. He will endeavour to delude you, to think yourself more righteous than others; taking God's office out of His hands, that he may bereave you of the efficacy of your labour, or sow some tares among your wheat making you delight in embracing a righteousness for some self end. For his tares are so like the true wheat, that it is hard to gather them out of it, unless you are well used to their taste. And as for your fervency for the Gospel of God in opposing all his assaults, for this he will stir up enemies both of your seeming friends and known enemies. If he cannot entice you to a false understanding of them, he will endeavour to screen your mind, to abuse your knowledge in the matter. If it be possible, hiding it from your discernment, but if he finds you so watchful that he cannot make a conquest of you, then he will try you further, if God permits; so as to put you in prison, or take away your life, for your fervent zeal for the Gospel.

But know that if you are brought that far, God will not leave you, though you may be under a cloud for a season; yet the sun will break through, expelling the darkness in an instant, yes, in a moment of time. Happy is he that overcomes all the rest, giving testimony of his fidelity in this to everyone, but I shall say more of this, deferring it at this time.

You must press forward still, you are not yet come to discern the difficulty of this in your urgent care. We will now discuss the greatest part of his enmity, in seeking to keep us from believing in the Captain of our Salvation, and in relying upon him for all our strength. He labours to deceive us in taking up this Weapon of Faith. So he will try to fix our minds on our own strength, trusting in our own conquests; he will leave no corner of your heart untempted, if he sees any possibility of getting within your walls under a pretence of friendship. The purpose is to deceive and rob you of this your weapon, as it is the chief weapon of our defence, which enables us to quench all his fiery darts. And so we keep our rare jewel from all his demonic delusions, for if he gets this shield of faith from you by any deceitful contrivance, he will make a conquest of you at his pleasure; knowing it is not for him to assault any that have this shield of faith in their hands for defence. I say, he cannot overthrow any of these by an ordinary way contrary to their way of worship, or stand maintaining pitched battle against such as have their faith truly grounded and fixed upon the love and strength of Christ Jesus.

But he does not lack flatteries, such as may seemingly sympathise with the true and grand emulations of the truth in show and profession, though it differs in their intent of doing it. Therefore, he that is a warrior in Christian warfare, must not only war against known waverings, but against seeming steadfastness, confidence and unmoveableness also. You must examine every thought that comes to you, trying it by the touch-stone of the word of God, before granting it admittance. If you do not take heed you may be deceived, for the Devil may appear in the likeness of an Angel of Light, doing many things you may think unlikely. He can be as faithful and religious as the Scribes and Pharisees; but he will not be willing that you should attribute anything to God as proceeding from him, or that you should seek his glory in performing it. Your faith must agree between event and effect, or it may be like the true faith, as the people of old cried, 'Peace, peace', when the LORD had not said it. Yes, his ends are so subtle, deceiving prophet and people: as he was subtle with the Scribes and Pharisees, for they gave the appearance of true faith in many respects. It was built on alms and the fulfilling of the Law, praying for success in it. But they gave their alms to be seen of men, and therefore they had their reward. They had the praise of men for their gifts, and as for regarding the Law, they were exact in many respects; as in paying tithes of mint, anise and cummin (Matthew 23:23).

Relieving the oppressed and pleading the cause of the needy, they took small care of that; making a conscience seemingly to God, as to pray often, and under pretence of religion, they would devour widows houses. Although they seemed religious in the sight of men, they were hardly religious in anything before God.

For it is not so easy as many seem to think it is, to be a Christian, or a Christ- like man. If you build your faith on any other Rock than Christ's death and Resurrection, then you are not engaged in this warfare; you cannot exercise faith without good warrant. I say, if you do not pull down and root up all other appearances not at one with this, holding that this proceeds from the same root and centre which the sufferings of Christ crown us with, you cannot exercise a faith with good warrant.

We shall not yoke ourselves with burdensome impediments in our Divine aspirations, for no clear eye can discern things so bright or Divinely manifested, much less believe them. True faith is not built on our own merits; but all such thoughts strike at the original ground of true faith, and is as contradictory an enemy to it as may be. Mark what the Apostle Paul says of true faith, 'Being justified freely by his grace through the redemption that is in Christ Jesus. Whom God hath set forth to be a propitiation through faith in his blood, to declare his righteousness for the remission of sins that are past, through the forbearance of God; To declare, I say, at this time his righteousness: that He might be just, and the justifier of him that believeth in Jesus' (Romans 3.24-26).

CHAPTER SIX

HOLINESS AND PURITY IN WORSHIP AND PRACTICE

Christ will not look upon you as partners in the grounds of your faith. He has conquered all such enemies that lead us captive at their will by His suffering for us, pacifying the Divine fury of His Father; being a propitiation to intercede with His Father for us. That He may reconcile all differences that hindered us from having a peaceable and complete union and oneness with our God. So that He may be our Father, as well as His Father, and our God, as well as His God; and that He might rejoice in us as brethren. Being united with Him, by what He has undergone for us; that we may jointly declare the manifold love of God, singing praises to His Name. This was the intent of Christ in interceding to the Father for us; only He would not have us slight His undertakings for us, so that we deceive ourselves. Do not dishonour His mockings, scoffings and deridings which He bore for our offences, when we should have eternally perished, had He not stepped in between our sin and His Father's wrath.

He did for us what we were not able to do for ourselves. So He will have us own Himself as 'the author and finisher of our faith' (Hebrews 12.2). You must, therefore, war against every appearance of evil, and everything that seeks to oppose this way of grounding your faith. But I shall leave this to your study, to examine how many such guests you entertain; thinking them to be your friends; as I intend speaking a word or two on the matter in some of my following discourse, if God permits.

And as you have resisted and must resist all the foregoing devices of this your envious, yet more subtle enemy, so you must engage against all his ways of ensnaring you in your charity. For he will not leave striving to conquer you by craft, if it is possible. He may see it is vain to tempt you in other ways; he will promise you great gain and content, yes, he will give you all the enticements and the allurements that the whole world can afford. He may persuade you that you can keep all these and be charitable; he does not care how fair a pretence you make of being charitable, but be sure of this, he will strike at the very root of it. Especially if it is used to God's glory, he will war against you, using your pride and self-seeking. You may as well lay down your weapons, as pretend to withstand him while you fortify him.

If we offer any praise to an imagined thing, that is due only to God, attributing more honour to it, esteeming it more than is due by God's appointment; this will be a hard saying for many professors to pass by, yet it is true. Jeremiah has a notable expression, to this purpose, the people would not be beaten down from burning 'incense to the queen of heaven' (Jeremiah 44.25). The people served their own imagination. As the Apostle said, 'there be gods many and lords many. But to us there is but one God, the Father, of whom are all things' (1 Corinthians 8.5,6). And as you read in another place, there are those who, 'worshipped and served the creature more than the Creator, who is blessed for ever. Amen' (Romans 1.25). He plainly expresses this in the foregoing verses: that they, 'changed the glory of the incorruptible God into an image like to corruptible man, and to birds and four-footed beasts; and creeping things' (Romans 1.23). Even as if the Apostle said, that they worshipped themselves, attributing the glory that was God's own by right, to themselves; and gloried in so doing, and delighted themselves in birds, and four-footed beasts, and creeping things more than in the Creator, from whom they had their being. Therefore he says, 'wherefore God also gave them up to uncleanness through the lust of their own hearts, to dishonour their own bodies between themselves'.[1] Be sure, that when they came to that degree of apostasy, God would not leave them without punishment for it, but lets them run into all unseemly behaviour, as you may read in verses 20, 30, and 31 of this chapter. When God gives up a people to their own lusts and desires of their own hearts, they run on from one degree of unrighteousness to another, till at last they are so captivated by their own lusts, that though they come to see that they act contrary to the rules of natural reason, yet they have no desire to leave it. Running on and persisting in one evil device to another; from committing fornication with their own lusts, to covetousness, malignity, and so to murder and debate, having no understanding that they become covenant breakers; as the Apostle says, they are 'without natural affection, implacable, unmerciful'(Romans 1:31).

[1] Romans 1.24; Ed.

Therefore, I say, beware of idolatry, and do not make it your business to worship these and such like gods. As the Apostle says plainly, 'Whose god is their belly, and whose glory is their shame' (Philippians 3.19). Fix your faith aright in God's prescribed rule, and then you will be able to wage war with the devil in his most cunning designs. But it will require your fervent care to continually watch, that you may be provided for at His coming.

For if you seek to do the will of the Father, which is *holiness and purity*, you must observe what His commands are. And do not think to secure yourselves by notional pretences and literal expressions, rudely reasoning with yourselves, in the worst of senses, accounting it a small sin to offend God; or to walk contrary to His commandments of *love and charity, peace and truth.*

If you walk contrary to this, you may profess what you please, but if your actions and intentions do not answer what your pretences seem to blaze out in your notional extremes, I will not value that opinion, though they pretend to be saints or angels. For if they walk so loosely, that their own hearts condemn them, much more will God condemn them, who sees and knows in secret. Happy is he that can try all things with Solomon, and yet not be linked in his affection to anything. I speak as in respect of his serving or idolising anything below God, he can rejoice with an heroic spirit, not only that devils are made subject to him, but that his name is written in the Book of Life. He can try and search into the secondary powers of the world, and yet not conclude with the heathen philosophers, that the images of them should be worshipped. Because as they say, they represent their gods to them, and the reverencing of God is uncovering of the head, or sprinkling with holy water; and exterior expiations, exterior ornaments for our Divine prayers, musical harmony, burning wax candles, ringing of bells, adorning temples, altars and images, in which they say, is required a special reverence and comeliness.

This is not a garden for such to plant their vine in, who by the Spirit of Jehovah can like the bee suck honey out of the thistle, accounting the honeysuckle the more rare flower. He that is truly grounded in this, will know what I mean in all the rest. It is not the sun, moon or any inferior light by which men walk or act, but acknowledge a more supreme and splendant brightness to be their guide in all things. They can try all these, making it experimentally appear that they seek the honour of Him which governs and rules all things, even as He pleases, and when He pleases to alter them? They are made subject to Him at all times, yes, He gives them a brighter splendour at one time than at another to our view. And what is the glory of anything, but in the manifestation of it? Oh! happy is he that like a bee can go to thistles and suck virtue out of them, as well as from the sweetest flowers, though they are more estimable in their sight. It argues the spirit of discerning, as well as the spirit that tries and searches. He needs not fear being deceived that knows honey when he tries it, much less he that knows it by sight; he will like the wasp lie prying after the bees nest, when he can suck the purest out of the flower. If there is a more bitter sting in the nest than he has power to expel: as snake commonly keeps both bee and wasp away, though they all have stings. Let this be our observation, that the lesser must be swallowed up by the greater, or else be put to flight; thrice happy is he that is truly conquered by the swallower-up of all things.

He can plead a true and certain interest with any man or all men, for whatever grows of itself is readily engrafted into this stock. It abides, though the winter frosts may seemingly eclipse the beauty of our professions, yet it cannot reach our root. But we shall retain so much sap, as will cause our branches to flourish again in due season. As the philosophers conclude, the sun will not spend all his year in a sign [the same state], where he has his detriment or fall, but will by his progressive motion in his exactness, in his line or circuit, go straight forward, and does not look backward. As though he was afraid of those captivating powers, as I may say, having dominion over him at such times, as is apparent in our horizon. The power he assures himself of in March, he is deprived of in September, and that glorious show of heat, yes, even to scorch us by in July, is overswayed by the unequal frequenting of a January approach. Yet, they say, the sun continues going forward still, notwithstanding all the repulses of his most potent enemies.

Even so, he that really honours the work of grace, and the benefit of his endeavours, that Christ has purchased for all them that will believe and lay hold upon Him in His death and resurrection; I say, such a one that is truly sensible of what worth and value Christ's death and life has to all those that enjoy a portion of it, effectually operating over all the impediments that are in the way to hinder his true discerning of it; he cannot but press forward. He accounts himself happy in each step he adds to his journey; in this he discerns that he gets [gains] ground. You need not urge such a one to be wary, for he cannot but discern when he gets [gains] ground, and when he loses it. For if anyone speaks well of him and assures him of peace, yet if he searches and finds any corner of [his] heart not swept, be sure he will not cry peace to himself. He will take the bosom of righteousness and truth, and will carefully sweep it out, making all clean within, for he cannot sleep in quiet until he has got his house clean.

As no earthly man can take his rest when he knows that there is a thief within his house, that will take all advantage to rob him, but will rather lock up his chiefest jewels, that they may not be taken from him, if he cannot get him out of the house. Though they are securely locked, and there be no thief in the house, yet if he has any treasure that he takes much delight in, he will be watchful; lest anyone should break into his house unexpectedly, bereaving him of that in which he delights.

Even so, a discerning Christian that knows there is a thief within his house, he cannot but dread the worst of things, so long as any suspected enemy is within his confines. But if he knows there is none, and has tried them all thoroughly, yet he will stand upon his watch, keeping his doors locked about him (when he is at home or abroad). He is wary with whom he confers as associates sit for his result; whether he is with the LORD at home, or in the turba[2] of his mind, he will be watchful that 'a stranger doth not intermeddle with his joy' (Proverbs 14:10). Depriving him of that enjoyment by which he can convey his soul to its most fixed bliss. No man can beat him off of this watchfulness, when he has once tasted the love of God, so as to witness that he is satisfied with it. Not that I think it is enough to seem satisfied or talk of being satisfied, but I speak of them who are really satisfied. You have a notable text of scripture in John, when Christ tells the woman of Samaria that, 'whosoever drinketh of the water that I shall give him shall never thirst' (John 4.14). And later He tells the Jews. 'your fathers did eat Manna in the wilderness, and are dead. This is the bread which cometh down from heaven, that a man may eat thereof, and not die. I am the living bread, which came down from heaven: if any man eat of this bread, he shall live for ever.'[3]

Many taste of this bread in some measure in many degrees, and yet never stand upon their watch, to keep dogs from eating it out of their mouths, and carrying it out of their sight.

[2] From the latin, *turbae*: a musical term which denotes the chorus sung in a religious oratario or passion, i.e. the chorus of Handel's 'Messiah.' Ed.

[3] John 6:49-51; Ed.

Bringing them some of their old diet, even garlic and onions: these are such as were taken in the parable for the stony ground 'where they had not much earth: and forthwith they sprung up, because they had no deepness of earth; and when the sun was up, they were scorched'[4]. Some 'brought forth plentifully' even for the harvest. Therefore, I say, he that wars in this life, must be sure to watch when the enemy seeks to assault and batter down his walls; defaming his weapons and poisoning them with his intermingled seeming delights. He lies in wait to infect us, even as a fisher[man] lays bait to catch his intended prey.

So that you shall have baited hooks, such as you think very rare as agreeable to your disposition as may be, and to advance his own ends, he will fit you if possible with his variety of pleasant dainties. If you are persuaded to deal with him, he will deal for small profit rather than lose your acquaintance. If it be but making slight of your word; or self-conceitedness in your worship; or worshipping for custom; or believing because others say that it is true, when it may be you have no warrant in your own hearts that it is true. But because others say so, you will believe it, for you are sure that such men would not say so, if it were not so.

[4] Matthew 13:5,6; Ed.

Alas! my poor friends, you have no other ground for your faith than what another gives you; you satisfy yourselves with what others say, and do not enquire whether it is according to God's holy word. This is left for an example, you are far from knowing what you fix your faith upon. You will be like the children of Israel, who followed Moses, because they saw that God worked many miracles by him. But when Moses was longer on the Mount than they supposed he would stay, they were presently at a loss, and charged Aaron to make them a god to go before them (Exodus 32.1). They were under his preaching for forty years, and it is recorded of them, that they did not know the ways of God.

Many writers affirm them to be a peculiar people by their deserts, but I find no such thing recorded in Scripture. Therefore I shall speak what is manifest to me, though I know it will seem harsh to many, to believe what I here infer. But I would have them take notice, that it is one thing for a people to be made happy by obedience, and another to be made happy by God's infinite mercy and forgiveness.

Israel was made happy by God's love and compassion to them in the wilderness, but not by desert; there is a great difference between God's loving a people, and a people obeying God.

Therefore I desire everyone may seriously consider when they read or hear the occasion of the words spoken, and the time when it was spoken. And the dispensation[5] that the people were under when it was spoken, or what degree of faith the people were heirs of by knowledge, that it was effectually to be made theirs. For if your enemy can entrap you, he will soon be more potent, if it be possible; for he has an apple[6] for Eve, so to betray Adam, a discontented pride in Cain to bring him to murder Abel (Genesis 12), a fear in Abraham to make him deny that Sarah was his wife, a feast for Noah, to make him commit fornication with his two daughters, and a covetousness in Jacob to deny his brother for a mess of potage, unless he would assign him his birthright (Genesis 25). Afterwards he feared that God was not able to help him to the blessing of Isaac, without his deluding his old father, a pride for David, that he might number the people, and so displease his God (2 Samuel 24.1), and a lovely Delilah for Samson, that might take away his life (Judges 16).

I might supply several more of these his aforementioned stratagems and cunning devices which he has made use of, as is

[5] The particular religious system operating in the nation at that time. Ed.

[6] Often representing the forbidden fruit. Ed.

apparent in the Old Testament and New, to which I shall refer you. Happy is he that keeps his watch and stand closely armed, ready to answer him in any of his attempts. That he may rejoice over all his works, that has gained the victory by keeping close to the rule of his preserving and defending Saviour. Knowing that it is by His strength that he stands, by giving heed to the narrowest and most difficult of His commands, observing it merely for the glory of his Father. Knowing that he can in no way show himself to seek a kingdom that is not of this life, 'If we say that we have fellow-ship with Him, and walk in darkness, we lie and do not the truth' (1 John 1.6). Because he calls God Father, when he does not know God, neither does God own his actions.

There is a people whom I have heard much of, that when they are going about anything that they imagine, will hardly bear the taste of the Scripture, they will say, that they will enquire of God, whether they may do it or not. And through the strength of their desire of their own wills, draw the sense and intent of the Scriptures to what they please, or what pleases their fancy best. Thinking themselves secure enough, if they frame a prayer to God to direct them in it. Though it may be they will not listen to what God puts into their minds at that time, adhering rather to what is more beneficial, as they think, for their own ends. Not that they blot the Scripture clean out in show, but it seems difficult to them in such cases, and so will under a pretence of Religion, do those things which neither reason, equity nor Scripture bears them out in any testimony.

This is as much as if they should go to enquire of God, whether they might freely murder a man or not. And if their desire is drawn to it and in case God does not show them some sign or wonder, or presently pour down some judgement upon them, they should be free to do it.

This is a great delusion of the Devil, to draw any man's mind to prayer, for God to direct them in anything, when their minds are absolutely bent to do wickedness. I say, it is one of the highest provocations to provoke God's fury that you can invent, as the Scripture has it, the prayers of the wicked are 'an abomination to the LORD' (Proverbs 28.9). It is a thing too common in our days, for many men to content themselves with a form of prayer, when they do not understand even one petition of the enquiry, nor that the thing they ask to be according to the will of God or not, which He has left for our instruction. But they seek to bring the will of God to those things that stand to their benefit, and if they can keep themselves from the laws of men, taking hold of them, they think they shall be safe enough. They have the praise and applause of the great Rabbis of the times, looking no further; but Moses chose 'rather to suffer affliction with the people of God, than to enjoy the pleasures of sin for a season' (Hebrews 11.25).

But those that seek a kingdom in this world, take little or no care for their future joy, thinking it shall always go well with them. Because they imagine it is better with them than with the righteous at present, and they see no alteration. God's love is as much to them as to any sort of people, and they flourish as David says, 'like a green bay tree' (Psalm 37:35). They have no frowns from God, neither [do they] see any change, therefore they go on securely, persisting in their own ways, as the Psalmist has it, 'God shall hear and afflict them, even as he that abideth of old, Selah. Because they have no changes, therefore they fear not God' (Psalm 55.19).

It is not enough to think of being secure, because you see no change, God may let you alone for the time you live in this life; but be sure of this, you must come to give [an] account at the last day, where all your actions will be tried by the fire, to see if they stand. Whatever we have done in this life, must be brought before the judgement seat of God, where great mens words will not serve our turn, neither can our former friends bail us, but Justice will be Justice, and Mercy will be Mercy; God cannot lay either of them aside. Do not stay your minds upon the abilities of great men, or on the pretended friendship of any man, for it is your own conscience that must appear to excuse, or else accuse you. So I say, lose the friendship of all your seeming friends, rather than wrong your Chief friend. For if He is forced to be your enemy, He will do you more wrong than all your other friends can do you good. Setting Christ's sufferings aside, they will be of small or no effect to you, if you give admittance to any unrighteous guests. Therefore rather lose all the friendships that may seem to prefer you in this life; yes, even your right hand, than risk being shut out of heaven.

It is not any other friend, save your conscience, that must give an account of your actions in this life. It will lie upon yourself, either for good or evil, 'the kingdom of heaven is like unto a merchant man, seeking goodly pearls. Who when he had found one pearl of great price, went and sold all that he had, and bought it' (Matthew 13.45,46).

Even so, he that has ever experienced the

love of God, will leave his Father and Mother, and all other seeming friends, rather than lose this pearl, or act contrary to the truth. Yet Christ does not in any way advise children to be disobedient to their earthly parents in respect of their obedience, if it is possible to content them or obey them. Rather He advises them to be just obeyers of God, by keeping the Commandments of God; commanded to be kept in the presence of God and men. Not that anyone can imagine themselves to be an approved fulfiller of the Laws of God, so long as he acts unjustly between man and man.[7]

As I remember it was historically expressed in the judgement of some heathens concerning the opinion of the Christians, that they judged the God of the Christians not to be a good God, by reason of their unfaithfulness, one toward another, and their inhumane carriage towards them. It is a sad omen of conversion, when they that should become a pattern to others to walk by become a reproach and defame their God. Or rather the God of truth, in their actions

[7] Watson believed that we are saved by Christ alone, and then through our love toward Him, we endeavour by the help of the Spirit, to make the moral law (the Ten Commandments) our rule of life. The Law cannot save, but to deny that it is the rule of life for the believer, is to be an Antinomian. cf. Romans 6; Ed.

towards men; I never read that Christ or His Apostles left them any such example. Rather to approve themselves to be examples of the flock, and not lords over God's heritage, offering no offence 'neither to the jew or gentile' (1 Corinthians 10.32). But rather showing ourselves to be such as seek to glorify the name of God by our uprightness and exactness to man.

Even as it is recorded of the prophet Daniel, 'Then the presidents and princes sought to find occasion against Daniel concerning the kingdom; but they could find none occasion for fault; for as much as he was faithful, neither was there any error or fault found in him. Then said these men, 'we shall not find any occasion against this Daniel, except we find it against him concerning the law of his God' (Daniel 6.4,5). Faithfulness is a happy ornament, though they that wear it may be persecuted by men, yet they will be upheld by God.

Oh! let us not pretend to be spiritual walkers, when we have not acted the things that even moralists account no less than their duty to do. Lest we become heirs of that woe pronounced against the Scribes and Pharisees, for pretending to be more righteous than any sort of people in their time, 'and for a pretence make long prayer: therefore ye shall receive the greater damnation' (Matthew 23.14). And you know that you can in no way tempt God more, than praying to Him for selfish ends; you do no better than seek to pull a curse upon your own heads. But whenever you are directed to pray, take these three directions.

1. Desire with the help of God, to banish all self-ends, and self-aims. That you may come to understand the will of God in the Scriptures.

2. Consider really with yourself, that the thing that you desire, is not to the prejudice of anyone. But that you do as you would have others do to you, in case they were in your condition.

3. Be sure that you use as much mercy in your undertakings, as you would have God use to you on the Last Day. Then if you find that all these agree with your undertakings, you may expect an answer assuredly from the LORD, that is to say, a blessing.

For do but mind the strange appearances of men in our times, in their intercessions to God in prayer. One prays for the restoring of one thing; and another prays for the throwing of that thing down. One will persecute another because he will not worship God as he would have him worship Him; another will seek to take away the life of others, because they will not conform to what they conceive is the right way of worship. So religion may but be your cloak, you value not what rule you have for your actions.

Oh England, England,[8] have you forgotten what the prophet complained of, that they draw near God with their mouths, but their hearts are far from observing his ways.[9] Oh that I could cause you to understand the things which belong to your peace, before they are hidden from your eyes. Then surely you would own God to be a God of peace and love, and not such an imagined fancy as most men imagine Him to be. Then you would come to understand that obedience is a better sacrifice, and to hearken is better than the fat of rams.[10] And to cry, 'who then is Paul, and who is Apollos, but ministers by whom ye believed, even as the LORD gave to every man. I have planted, Apollos watered; but God gave the increase' (1 Corinthians 3.5,6).

[8] The author complains of the relativistic and intolerant religious practises in his day. The Church of England during Watson's lifetime witnessed violent swings, first toward godliness and then back to empty ceremonialism.

[9] Isaiah 29.13; Ed.

[10] I Samuel 15:22; Ed.

It is far better for us to leave off professing ourselves religious, than to pretend to a great height in religion and walk in the inhumane rudiments of the world. For whosoever will be a Disciple of Christ, must take up his cross and follow Him,[11] in the same ways He walked in. He must not turn back to fetch any self-end to carry along with him; for if he does, he will endanger being shut out of the Bride-chamber. Neither may he be freed from many encounters with the perverse enemy of mankind, but must take up his cross and march forward through persecutions, afflictions and crosses in this life. And the more he seeks to serve his Master, the more he will be disdained, not that any can tax him to injustice either to God or men. But wherever Christ has a church the Devil will be labouring to lay one stone or another, you may go on a great way, and build a very fair tabernacle with *mortal* stones, and have the love of men and not the hatred of the Devil. If you come to understand your task, what it is that you are to build, be sure he will seek to torment you, and make your wages as uncomfortable as he can. He will have a *Cain* to persecute *Abel*, and an *Ishmael* for *Isaac*, and an *Esau* for *Jacob*, and ten brethren against *Joseph*, and whole cities and nations against the Prophets and Apostles. He did not

[11] Matthew 16:24; Mark 8:34; Luke 19:23; Ed.

leave Christ untempted.

So that as I said before, if you will enter into this company to be one of their society, you must not think it too much to be a false prophet in the estimation of others. But as all your forerunners have done, count it your joy that you do not deserve it at their hands; though you are counted a magician with Moses and Daniel, or a worshipper of a contrary thing with most of the prophets. Or a changer of customs and a profane person, or a wine-bibber, or a madman, or a breaker of the Sabbath with Christ and his Apostles. Count it your joy to bear the reproach of these things, but be sure to keep yourselves free from deserving any of them. But approve yourselves to be His friends, by doing what He has commanded you, and then let the world rage, and the Devil spit his venomous poison how he pleases, God will provide you with that which expels it.

Whenever you are brought to the maturity of knowledge, as to experience the love of God as it is in Christ Jesus, you will not sell your birthright for all the seeming preferments and advancements, that any unrighteous tempter shall try to betray you with. Look at the branch, and you will most commonly find what it is that nourishes the root. If it is nourished by any inward spring, or grows by the riverside, it will flourish, although the showers of rain do not come as frequently as they used to. He that knows not how to suffer with Him, never knew how to rejoice with Him; and he that is His, knows how to do both.

But let not anyone mistake me in this, thinking that I conclude that everyone that suffers, must suffer for Christ. I must confess, I hardly ever read of any moralist that could suffer for what he maintained, if he could in any way prevent it. In case he could not avoid suffering, any man will rather choose that in which he has most experience, as a philosopher for his philosophy, or a Marshall for his adventures in war. But happy is he that can lay down his life as freely as keep it, on the account of his LORD and Master, in due respect to His honour and glory; and not for selfish ends or self-glory.

Many I know, will be harping at these expressions. But let them know, that as I conclude the Scriptures not to be void of reason, so I also conclude, that it is beyond the moral reason of men, to find out the depths of the Scriptures.

CHAPTER SEVEN

BUILDING THE TRUE TEMPLE OF GOD

As far as war is concerned, I must count it as a thing of fashion in our days,[1] and for me to seek to alter this fashion, I shall be liable to the censures of men. Yet let the Scriptures be true, and have the respect for them that you should have, and then let me be what you please. I shall be brief in this matter, only referring you to the words of Christ that He left with His disciples: 'Put up again thy sword into his pace: for all they that take the sword shall perish with the sword. Thinkest thou that I cannot now pray to my Father, and he shall presently give me more than twelve legions of angels? But how then shall the Scriptures be fulfilled, that thus it must be?' (Matthew 26:52-54). And the Apostle says, 'For the weapons

---

[1] During Watson's lifetime England was ravaged by two civil wars, fought between 1642-49. In the period even the godly in England and Scotland came into armed conflict against each other. (Ed.)

of our warfare are not carnal, but mighty through God to the pulling down of strong holds; casting down imaginations, and every high thing that exalteth itself against the know-ledge of God' (II Cor. 10:4,5). This is beyond the work of a moral sword: 'Endeavouring to keep the unity of the Spirit in the bond of peace.' (Eph. 4:3)

And in James, [we read]:

'From whence come wars and fightings among you? Come they not hence, even of your lusts that war in your members? Ye lust, and have not: ye kill and desire to have, and cannot obtain: ye fight and war, yet ye have not, because ye ask not. Ye ask, and receive not, because ye ask amiss, that ye may consume upon your lusts. Ye adulterers and adulteresses, know ye not that the friendship of the world is enmity with God? Whosoever therefore will be a friend of the world, is the enemy of God' (James 4:1-4).

And you will also read in the first book of Chronicles, 'But God said unto me, Thou shalt not build an house for my name, because thou hast been a man of war, and hast shed blood' (I Chronicles 28:3).

So if that type of the true Temple could not be built by blood; surely the true Temple of

God cannot be built by blood or war, but in peace. It is not that Egypt is righteous enough to build the Temple of the LORD, though they may be a scourge to Edom, as Nebuchadnezzar was to Israel. I will not accuse a defensive sword, because I have seen that the manifestations of God are not all revealed to one man; but I cannot find that any disciple of Christ should use a moral sword.[2] He that is a disciple of Christ is a builder of the true Temple; for he that is a builder of the true Temple should not take revenge against his enemies, but commit his cause to the LORD, to whom vengeance belongs. Therefore Christ bids us to forgive our enemies, lest we should seek vengeance where God seeks none; for we are apt to condemn where God justifies, and set ourselves upon His seat.

[2] Pacifism is not being advocated in this passage. The author distinguishes between the legitimate defensive war and the use of a 'moral sword.' Pacifism had no Biblical basis for the puritans and the concept of a defensive war or just war had gained acceptance within Christianity since Augustine of Hippo, in the 5th century. However, the suggestion that the Church could proselytize by force, was justified by some as a 'moral cause.' One clear historical illustration of this thinking were the Crusades launched against Islam, in the late 11th century and beyond; these were a direct result of Papal power and were waged by an apostate Church, namely Rome. (Ed.)

Where are any of God's messengers that have not received this censure from the men of their times? Therefore, lest we should be liable to this failing, Christ warns us not to judge our brethren, lest we be judged; for to his own Master he stands or falls.[3] We are forbidden to judge, according as it appears in John, 'Judge not according to the appearance, but judge righteous judgement' (John 7:24). As no man can judge by appearance in many things, without doubting whether he judges rightly. Therefore, as we cannot measure God's love, let us forbear judging ourselves to be better than others, lest we undervalue Christ's sufferings.

But as concerning an offensive war, I find no grounds in the Scriptures for it; and if any man can show me any Scripture for it since the death of the testator, at which time the Testament was in force, I shall not take it ill at his hands. For I have not so learned Christ as to flatter anyone: 'He that speaketh flattery to his friends, even the eyes of his children shall fail' (Job 17:5). And in Proverbs [we learn], 'Open rebuke is better than secret love. Faithful are the wounds of a friend, but the kisses of an enemy are deceitful' (Proverbs 27:5,6).

But someone may object why did Christ not bid the soldiers to lay down their arms? They came to Him to ask what they should do, and He did

[3] Matthew 7:1-5; Ed.

not discourage them in their undertaking; but He bids them to do violence to no man, and be content with their wages.

I answer that any man that is a perfect performer of this part of his duty, may give a just account of his actions. But you must observe that He who advises them, also commands them that they should love their enemies, 'bless them that curse you, and do good to them that hate you, and pray for them that despitefully use you, and persecute you; that ye may be the children of your Father which is in Heaven' (Matthew 6:44,45).

But I suppose that Christ never advised any of His disciples to go to war with the worst of His enemies, nor to fight for a kingdom of this world. Rather suffering by the men of this world, if one must. And as for His advice to the soldiers, it was rather that they should not break their engagements respecting their governors, or their loyalty to their promise, rather than owning war to be according to the will of God. For those for whom they fought were such as Christ condemns as mere worldlings. Therefore, how could their cause be good? Yet He would not advise them to break their engagements [contracts], but to act truthfully, that those whom He spoke against for doing injustice, might not have anything to accuse Him of, in neither His advice nor action.

CHAPTER EIGHT

THE COVENANT OF GRACE

What difference is there between the righteous and the wicked, but only in their actions, as in respect of their honouring or dishonouring God? It is a very vain thing for anyone to think they are spiritually righteous, when they are not morally just. How can any man spiritualize himself and not use morality? For whatever is manifested to be acted between man and man, is external, in respect of non-continuance. Therefore God expects that as you have received a talent of righteousness and truth, so you should act in truth and deal justly with all men. Not boasting of a talent of truth and righteousness when you act contrary [to it], but abuse its true use. God is better pleased in the just demeanor toward men, than with thousands of sacrifices by your pretences in religion.

This is demonstrated in the case of the Children of Israel in the time of Joshua. As you may read in Joshua 9.19, they could not kill the Gibeonites because they had made a promise, that they would not destroy them. Although the LORD had commanded them to destroy all those people and places, showing them the danger of making a league with them, as you may read in Deuteronomy [chapter] 7.

Oh! How would many in our day swallow such an oath, and never think themselves the worse for so doing. Should such a thing extend to their own ends in any one particular, these people might have pleaded that they could not disobey the commands of the LORD, who had commanded them to destroy both young and old. They entered into an oath with them on no other account, but as a people that lived at a distance from the place, which God had given them. It would be a great danger for their sons marrying with their daughters, and their daughters with the Gibeonites, and so entice them to follow other gods.

Therefore, being forewarned by the LORD, they would prevent the worst, being it was upon a spiritual account; as indeed it seems with our most zealous professors. But the Princes of Israel say they may not do it, for they had entered into a covenant with them, to let them live. Therefore, they would not become covenant-breakers; but would make a covenant to be a covenant in deed as well as in words. I will show you three reasons why the Princes of Israel would not break this covenant, when the people earnestly desired it.

1. In respect that they had not broken the command of God willingly or knowingly, and in case they should seek to break this league with the Gibeonites, they should offend against Him in both, for the God that bid them to keep those covenants and commands, tells them to act justly and to lie not, one to another. That they may demonstrate to all people that they worship a God of order and a God that will not lie. Seeing they could not keep both but were circumvented in one, they would be as exact as they could in the other. Many look at what God says in one respect, but not at others; it had [would have] been good if Israel had not entered into league with them, but on the contrary, to have destroyed them. But they had; though it was on account of strangers. Indeed, they asked them if they did not live amongst them, and they said they came from a far country.[1]

I fear that very few professors in our time would be so exact in their carriage, for the praise of their Master.

2. They knew they should very much dishonour their God in not confiding that He was able to keep their sons and daughters from believing or worshipping the gods of the heathen. If they should marry one with another

[1] Joshua 9:9; Ed.

it would seem a very dishonourable part for Israel, when they engaged [contracted] to Gibeon to break their covenant, for fear the Gibeonites should draw them or their sons from worshipping that God whom they served. It must needs argue that they gave evident witness, that their God is not strong enough to encounter the god of the heathens, and that is the way to worship a god that is not. In case you are engaged, I find no grounds in Scripture that you should ever falsify your word to others, being worse than you; for that is the way to make yourself worse than they.

Whereas if Gibeon lives with Israel, who knows but Israel may convert Gibeon; however Israel will be Israel so long as they keep this in mind. It was the opinion of an ancient heathen, that no man could be spiritually good, if he was not morally just; and his reason was that the spiritual God was a God of order.

But someone may object, suppose those that I have engaged to should give me any just occasion to break my covenant, they being as deeply engaged as I was, become covenant-breakers and not I. Hopefully I may break mine without wronging my conscience at all.

I answer, it is one thing to be found an offender in the sight or judgement of men, or their customary institutions, and another to be found an offender in the Last Day before the just Judge of heaven and earth. The laws of men may be clear to you, and so you cannot be said to be an offender of them; but if you approve yourself not guilty of refusing the advice of Christ and His Apostles you must look beyond the laws of men. In some things the laws of nations differ. Many kingdoms allow that which others condemn, but God is one entire being, and His Law the one edifying truth; which teaches us not to render evil for evil, but contrariwise good.

Suppose you are engaged conditionally, even by indenture,[2] where there are obligations laid upon both sides, and your partner breaks his part of the obligation, you cannot but account it evil in him. And will you commit the same evil by breaking your part, when you condemn the same thing in another? Christ advises us, that if any compel us to go with him one mile, to go two; and if any man strike you on the one cheek, turn to him the other, you shall not answer for this offence, but for your own. I must confess, it is my opinion that no-one can with any safety break their engagements from the time they stood engaged at first, though you may receive great injuries by the other parties default.

[2] Historically this was a sealed agreement, or contract, legally binding both parties to fulfill certain obligations towards each other. (Ed.)

The Apostle Peter plainly intimates as much in his first letter, 'for this is thankworthy, if a man for conscience toward God endure grief, suffering wrongfully. For what glory is it, if, when ye be buffeted for your faults, ye should take it patiently? But if, when ye do well, and suffer for it, ye take it patiently, this is acceptable with God' (I Peter 2:19,20). The Apostle does not advise the servant to break his covenant to his master, because the master breaks his, but rather suffer what punishment the master shall inflict upon him. Yes, herein is a believer's joy that he is accounted worthy to suffer for maintaining the truth in any one particular. For all are not called to suffer in one manner or way, though flesh and blood may not seem satisfied with it, by reason of the present anguish of spirit. For, 'no chastening for the present seemeth to be joyous, but grievous: nevertheless, afterward it yieldeth the peaceable fruit of righteousness' (Hebrews 12:11). So that though it seem to terrify your outward man, yet your inward man will be strengthened, which ought to be nourished [rather] than neglected. Though it may seem to prove disadvantageous to you in this life, yet here will be your joy, that you have obeyed the truth and can look death in the face with great boldness; by your exactness in your word to all men, as David speaks in Psalm 15, concerning those that shall be inhabitants in Zion, among which one thing is found needful. That is, to keep his word, 'He that sweareth to his own hurt, and changeth not' (Psalm 15:4).

Revenge belongs to the Lord. If you receive any wrong, commit your cause to Him and do not seek any revenge upon any man. But let no man seek to circumvent me in my description, I put a difference between the people of God promising, and a people that are in darkness. I speak of them that engage [contract] while they are in the tuition of the Lord, or at least own themselves to be, and a difference between the promises of the Law, or under the Law, as they were understood, and the differences under the gospel. Under the Law any man might put away his wife, only giving her a bill of divorcement; but Christ tells us that it is adultery to do it in the gospel. Causing those to commit adultery also, that are put away in that nature. So it is not everything that is customary with men, that is justifiable in the sight of God.

3. Israel had experienced that God made it His desire to keep those engagements that He had made to them, as it is often mentioned in the Scriptures, though they had broken their engagements as to their particular and general

failings. Yet God was so tender, lest He should break his part, that He does as it were stand and mediate before He insists upon any urgent or austere punishment. And He often invites them to return and review their ways, turning to repentance for their backsliding, that He may have mercy on them and defer his anger. God is just and merciful and it cannot be said of Him, that He ever broke any engagement to any person or people, for His promises have been to His people many times but [only] conditionally.

For as He engages to be a God and defender to them, if they will keep His Laws and observe to do His commands, so likewise He often engages that if they will not keep His Law, or perform their part, that He will punish them. Leaving them to their own wills and their own desires, and let[ting] them go on in their own filthiness, until they have fulfilled the desires of their own ways. Then He will take the rod and scourge them. So, as I said before, God is as just in performing this part of His Covenant, as He was [in] performing the other. By reason of the entailment of truth that did force Him to it, in respect to those promises, which are absolute, He is so exact in keeping them where there is no entailment to the contrary. He will keep His word though a people offend Him and vex His Holy Spirit, as seen in his promise to Abraham, Isaac and Jacob, in relation to His causing their seed to inherit the land of Canaan. Although His people oftentimes offended and vexed His Holy Spirit, nevertheless, He being a God of Truth would not be moved so far as to make His promise null and void of effect.

As He had promised that He would render up the only Beloved of His delight, His Son Jesus Christ, to the mercies of wicked men, even to do with Him after the imaginations of their own hearts, as far as concerned life to their appearance, so he fulfilled to the full. Although they had denied to own Him in His intercessions, for a condescension of love and unity. Yes, they did not own [confess] Him to be their God; they would have none of Him or His instructions. Beating His messengers, imprisoning and killing His Prophets, showing Him all the inhumane respect that they possibly could, dishonouring Him as much as lay in their power.

Nevertheless, God has promised that He would provide an acceptable sacrifice for the seed of Abraham, 'a lamb without blemish or spot.'[3] Though the people were so wicked and inhumane, breakers of all the Ordinances, Laws and Commands that He had given them to observe and do; yet He could do no less than perform His

[3] Genesis 22:8; I Peter 1:19; Ed.

promise. Otherwise how could it be said that He was a God of truth?

So it is plainly understood, that God has been compelled by truth many times, to bestow His gracious favours and mercies upon His people when they have deserved a curse. Oftentimes though it might with true acknow-ledgement and obedience become a blessing to them that receive it: so it proves to those that are obstinately bent, even a curse by their not prizing of it as they ought to do. Even as Christ was to Judas and several other Jews.

Besides, the Israelites dare not break their promise with Gibeon, for fear of dishonouring their God. Provoking Him to anger, by making him odious in the sight of the heathen, who do hold of this judgement; that if they promise anything, their gods will afflict them if they do not effect it. The very heathen would condemn their god of injustice, as indeed it was Jacobs answer to his sons Simeon and Levi, 'Ye have troubled me to make me to stink among the inhabitants of the land, among the Canaanites, and the Perizzites: and I being few in number, they shall gather themselves together against me, and slay me; and I shall be destroyed and my house' (Genesis 34:30). Jacob accounted it a greater offence for Simeon and Levi to break their covenant, than to let their sister remain with Hamor. Indeed, she had been the occasion of working the defam[ation] of Israel, even so, they had made Israel to stink before the nations on the other side, and so consequently [dishonoured] the God of Israel.

And if you mark the following chapter you will find that God takes notice of it in the first verse. God calls to Jacob, 'Arise, go up to Bethel, and dwell there' (Genesis 35:1). Turning back to chapter 28, you will find what Jacob promised in Bethel, where he is commanded to return. That is, his promise in Bethel, 'And Jacob vowed a vow, saying, if God will be with me, and will keep me in this way that I go, and will give me bread to eat, and raiment to put on, so that I come again to my father's house in peace; then shall the Lord be my God' (Genesis 28:20,21). Now God had performed His promise, but Jacob had failed in his, in that his sons had broken their covenant with Shecham and Hamor.

Objection: But what does God call Jacob to go to Bethel to do? Or to [demand the fulfillment of] his promise in Bethel?

Answer: It was to take notice that Jacob had broken his promise. And therefore, He commands Jacob to build an altar there, for he would not answer him on that altar, *Israel,* or in the breaking of the covenant, but in Bethel. [There] he owns [confesses] Him as his own God. Therefore, Jacob's first work was to cleanse his house of idols, as you may read in Genesis 35, and to bury them in Shecham, before he could go up to Bethel. And he tells his family that they must change their garments, 'arise, and go up to Bethel; and I will make there an altar unto God, who answered me in the day of my distress' (v. 3). By that means [such] a terror was struck into the hearts of the neighbouring cities, that they journeyed safely.

Secondly, Israel had purchased God's displeasure not long before this engagement [contract or covenant] was made with the Gibeonites, as seen in Joshua [chapter] 7: 'Israel hath sinned, and they have also transgressed my covenant which I commanded them: for they have even taken of the accursed thing, and have also stolen, and dissembled also, and they have put it even among their own stuff. Therefore the children of Israel could not stand before their enemies' (vv. 11,12).

So you see plainly, that God is very exact to have Israel keep His Law and Commandments. And had they not entered into covenant with the Gibeonites to let them live, they dare not have preserved any of their lives. But seeing they had engaged [covenanted] to do it, though it was unknown to them of their living in that place, God was more pleased than if they had broken their covenant. And Gibeon is not the last in the process of time that laid their helping hand to build the Temple of the LORD in Judah, as you have in Nehemiah. God was well pleased with Israel for keeping their covenant, in accepting the Gibeonites into His favour for Israel's sake. Whereas Achan offended against Him when there was no obligation to urge him to it, he will not be a friend with him or with Israel, until they have destroyed him. But Israel must fall before the men of Ai, and those that have not offended with polluting themselves in forbidden enticements. Therefore it is not that men always fall before their enemies for the sins that they commit. But for the pollution of others Israel is said to sin in that one had sinned, [namely] Achan. And God would suffer even 36 of the Israelites to die before the men of Ai, and the rest to flee for Achan's offence.

Therefore I would entreat every man that professes to be a Christian, to take heed of offending God in this, or any other thing. For surely if God does not take up a controversy against us for our backsliding, we may be the occasion of His fury against others who are more innocent than ourselves. God will not be a friend with Israel till the Babylonish garment is burned, and Achan stoned.

Look at it as well as you please, you know your pay will be according to your work. I need not tell you that there are more Babylonish garments than one, and I fear that some who profess high notions, have clothed themselves with them from the crown of the head to the sole of the foot; only wearing a religious cloak over it to deceive. Oh men! Look well to yourselves, and let not your own hearts condemn you before God. I will not condemn you, but I speak my mind plainly, for there are too many that heal your wound only too slightly, even as Jeremiah complained, 'They have healed also the hurt of the daughter of my people slightly, saying, Peace, peace; when there is no peace' (Jeremiah 6:14).

So it has plainly appeared in our time, that we have pretended to a great measure of light in Religion. But where is the man that cried, "we have fallen short?" But rather accounting that the judgement that is fallen upon you, O England, belonged to Rome and the Beast,[4]

[4] Watson referred in passing to the Reformed view of the rise of Antichrist. The prophecy in Daniel 8:9, II Thessalonians 2 and Revelation 17 were fulfilled in the

looking only for Christ's reign in person, not minding to set up his power in our hearts. Just as the Children of Israel thought themselves happier in the land of Canaan, whilst they were in the Wilderness, than they did in the pleasure of God, by which they were to enjoy it. And so they took to murmuring and repining at God's dealing with them according to His pleasure. Therefore He slew that generation of men, and would not suffer them to enter the land at all.

So I may say of you, O England, that has had more discourse on the throwing down of Babylon, than you have had zeal to the God that will throw Babylon down into the bottomless pit. If pretences could have done it, I must confess you might have gone a great way in it, but you sought to *cleanse only the outside;* and did not furbish the inside to answer it. It would be a very small satisfaction to you, to have Christ reign for a thousand years upon the Earth, and to begin in His reign before He has been lifted up in your heart. Therefore, 'seek first the kingdom of God and his righteousness; and all

Roman Catholic Church and the Papal usurpation of the Headship of Christ in the Church. Notwithstanding that manifest spiritual wickedness, the author protested against the danger of anyone trusting in an outward profession of the gospel rather than having a genuine soul saving faith in Christ.

these things shall be added unto you.'[5] And do not think to dwell with the Father, unless you eat the flesh of the Son, 'He that eateth my flesh and drinketh my blood, dwelleth in me, and I in him. As the living Father hath sent me, and I live by the Father: so he that eateth me, even he shall live by me' (John 6:56,57).

Therefore do not think of satisfying yourselves with anything below Him, but be sure to eat that which the Scriptures do manifest to be in Him. Thus wishing the one Almighty and infinite Being to direct you, and I, that we not look at things as they appear ordinarily, but as they are in reality and truth. That we may believe in Him who is our peace, 'add to your faith virtue, and to virtue knowledge; and to knowledge temperance; and to temperance patience; and to patience godliness; and to godliness brotherly kindness; and to brotherly kindness charity. For if these things be in you, and abound, they make you that ye shall neither be barren nor unfruitful in the knowledge of our LORD Jesus Christ' (II Peter 1:5-8). 'For so is the will of God, that with well doing ye may put to silence the ignorance of foolish men: as free, and not using your liberty for a cloke of maliciousness, but as the servants of God' (I Peter 2:15,16). If

[5] Matthew 6:33; Ed.

you have so learned Christ, as to observe and do these things that you are invited to, you need not fear what man can do unto you. But you will get into a strong harbour and take your repose, and wait till you hear the voice of the Bridegroom, crying, 'Come my people, enter thou into thy chambers, and shut thy doors about thee: hide thyself as it were for a little moment, until the indignation be overpast' (Isaiah 26:20).

Finis

Crook in the Lot

A Puritans understanding of
that thorn in your side
Thomas Boston

Introduced by J.I. Packer

In an revealing prologue, J.I. Packer shows how Boston's advice remains deeply relevant today. Boston was not preaching merely from his theological understanding, he was speaking from direct personal experience. Boston had real 'thorns' to deal with himself, ranging from his wife's paralyzing depression to his own experiences living for years with what were probably kidney stones. Thomas Boston was renowned for his clearly understood English and the manner in which he maintained that clarity while conveying messages of great depth. He brings his own unique combination of wonderfully profound and yet immensely practical advice to bear to give us a work of lasting impact.

> *'...the pure biblical wisdom of The Crook in the Lot is badly needed by many of us, and so I am delighted that it is being made available again in this handy form. For truly, as Americans love to say, this is where it's at.'*

J.I. Packer

ISBN 1-85792-178-X

The
Mortification of Sin
A Puritan's View of How to Deal with Sin in Your Life

John Owen
Introduction by J.I. Packer

The Mortification of Sin
*A Puritan's View on how to
Deal With Sin in Your Life*
John Owen

Introduced by J.I. Packer

John Owen insisted on the importance of Christians dealing effectively with their sinful tendencies and attitudes. He believed that God, through his Word and Spirit, had provided the guidelines and the power for this to be achieved.

In this book, John Owen effectively dismisses various excuses for not engaging in self-scrutiny and yet avoids the current trend of self-absorption. In so doing he provides principles to help believers live lives of holiness.

J I Packer, one of the best-known contemporary writers and theologians who re-introduced the Puritans to the modern church, provides a fascinating introduction to this book.

> *'I owe more to John Owen than to any other theologian, ancient or modern, and I owe more to this little book than to anything else he wrote.'*
>
> **J.I. Packer**

ISBN 1 85792 1070

CHRISTIAN
HERITAGE

THE ART OF MANFISHING

A Puritan's view of Evangelism

Thomas Boston
Introduced by J.I. Packer